Digital Talent Management

"This is an innovative and timely book which draws on leading edge research to provide important knowledge and insights into the distinctive challenges of managing digital talent, an emerging issue across the globe. The author team consisted of academics and practitioners, which provided a broader and deeper understanding of issues relating to digital talent.

I would highly recommend the book both for researchers and managers seeking to enhance their knowledge of digital talent."

—Hugh Scullion, *Hull University Business School, Hull University, UK*

"As digital transformation sweeps through many industries, company CEOs have quickly turned their attention to the digital competences they need and how they are going to get them. Whilst digital competence development is going to be crucial in this transformation, the attraction and retention of digital talent and their highly sought-after skills is likely to be a key priority on top management team agendas for some time to come. This inevitably requires answers to important questions such as who or what is digital talent, to what extent are they different from other types of talent, how to attract these individuals with a compelling employee value proposition, and how to retain them when many of their skills are transferable and employment opportunities will grow exponentially.

This book addresses these key questions and is a very timely contribution to both research and practice on the emerging area of digital talent management."

—Adam Smale, *Dean of the School of Management, University of Vaasa, Finland*

"The digital revolution will come and cover all areas of life. It will serve people, but in no way will it be able to function without them. There is already a great number of talent today that is very digitally minded and creates solutions. We need to connect them to the real world through social leadership skills. This book shows an optimised way of dealing with factual digital issues through people who know how to combine this levelheadedness with human leadership qualities. These new qualities need to be developed and enhanced to create a human-centred future, and are necessary to manage talent sustainably over the long term. Talent leaves when they do not feel gratitude or expectations are not met.

Anyone who is interested in a digital talent-friendly future, and wants to help shape it, should read this book."

—Michael Friemel, *Chief Executive Officer, CSS AG, Germany*

"This book is a must read for leaders in companies who are active in the digitization of our world. Here you can learn how to manage 'digital talent'—the foundation of all successful organizations in the future."

—Swen Rehders, *Managing Partner, NTT DATA Germany GmbH*

"Digital development is inevitable and it challenges organizations to succeed in digital transformation. This success is dependent on 'digital talent.' This fresh book surveys this new kind of talent for a new kind of talent management for a new kind of world, a world marked by COVID-19. It provides practical insights for meeting the requirements of a changing workplace. Both scholarly and practical, it has a clear and powerful message for company CEOs, HR managers and business schools across the globe."

—Johanna Hämäläinen, *Talent Development Lead, Marine Systems, Wärtsilä Finland*

Sorin Dan • Diana Ivana
Monica Zaharie
Daniel Metz • Mihaela Drăgan

Digital Talent Management

Insights from the Information Technology and Communication Industry

palgrave
macmillan

Sorin Dan
University of Vaasa InnoLab
Vaasa, Finland

Monica Zaharie
Babeş-Bolyai University
Cluj-Napoca, Romania

Mihaela Drăgan
Babeş-Bolyai University
Cluj-Napoca, Romania

Diana Ivana
Babeş-Bolyai University
Cluj-Napoca, Romania

NTT DATA
Cluj-Napoca, Romania

Daniel Metz
NTT DATA
Cluj-Napoca, Romania

Babeş-Bolyai University
Cluj-Napoca, Romania

ISBN 978-3-030-76749-5 ISBN 978-3-030-76750-1 (eBook)
https://doi.org/10.1007/978-3-030-76750-1

This Palgrave Macmillan imprint is published by the registered company Springer Nature Switzerland AG.
The registered company address is: Gewerbestrasse 11, 6330 Cham, Switzerland

Preface

"Their never-resting mind operates at an extraordinarily high level of abstraction.

They have very specific fields of interest and prefer to use graphic and comparative representation of objects.

Digital talent works daily in front of screens combining symbols such as '1, 0, (,), {,},;?' according to rules that change annually or more frequently. They do this aiming to enable the staff working in human resources, finance, and other management fields to have an interface which is easy to understand and use for managing their information and data.

Digital talent is up to date with the latest technologies, programming languages, and has specific information about niche projects, new start-ups and so forth. Talent in general, by contrast, prefers to stay up to date with Netflix, news, media, or the weather forecast.

They are valuable, and they know it well. Their financial expectations are greater than those of professionals and managers who work in other roles and tasks because they have one of the most difficult jobs in the world, they bring in large amounts of money and remain insufficient on the market.

Since they know they are valuable, they may seem picky and arrogant when it comes to living standards and work conditions. They know their rights very well and refuse to accept less than what they deserve.

They are overwhelmed with work and with the pressure to know everything that is required by their clients, whose ever-changing demands pressure them to start their work all over again.

Some digital talent can be difficult to manage. They thrive in silence, while technically optimal skills are a must.

The offer must be attractive:

- Top-notch computer;
- Good workspace with plenty of natural light;
- High-speed internet that operates at constantly high parameters;
- As many professional development opportunities as possible;
- Flexible hours;
- Home office—the most appreciated benefit;
- Flat hierarchy when it comes to communication;
- Interesting projects and novel technologies, and
- Likelihood to actively get involved in project development and the company as a whole.

When they are unhappy with something, they can say it out loud and with no diplomacy. The biggest mistake one can make is to restrict in any way the freedom of expression of a person whose intelligence and creativity are far above average. We need to let them speak their mind. The managerial approach demanding a predefined number of codes to be written or problems to be solved by a specific deadline is utopic given that, in digital works, contrary to what many people believe, you can write an entire code in just one moment of inspiration, after months of painful failure. What helps, instead, is a realistic approach that includes performance assessment over a certain period of time, but without a daily monitoring of execution times and of the actual hours spent in front of the computer.

Digital talent constantly challenges us all:

- To be organized;
- To know what we want and how to ask for it;
- To speak kindly to our team even when team members make mistakes;
- To appreciate the value of our team;
- To surrender control and try instead to guide our people—allowing their creativity to unleash;
- To listen to the ideas of our staff;
- To provide constructive feedback; and
- To regularly thank our team members for their efforts."

Dr. Daniel Metz, Chairman of the Board of Directors, NTT DATA Romania

The digital world is making more and more inroads into the various dimensions of human existence, and the world of work, organizational life and human resource management make no exception. Whether a blessing or a curse, this digital development appears to be inevitable. Like a train going on a one-way track, it goes farther and farther and becomes increasingly distant from the point of departure. When it comes to the future, the sky is the limit. Many reasons and motivations, either express or implied, can explain this propensity toward the digital realm that has culminated in the current Fourth Industrial Revolution (Industry 4.0). Automation, assisted by smart technologies, machine-to-machine communication and the internet of things, is expected to deepen the digital trend, leading to processes and activities that require less and less human intervention.

In this dynamic, complex and complicated sphere, it is easy to leave out an essential piece of the puzzle—the people who build this world. They may not have the power to orchestrate it, and consequently, they might not be the drivers behind it, but their hands—or more accurately—their minds, help to engineer, maintain and develop this world further day by day. They represent what this book refers to as 'digital talent', that is, a wide spectrum of information and communication technology (IT&C) professionals and managers who possess digital abilities, competencies and skills that are in high demand on the labor market globally. The products of their minds are typically immaterial and can be stored in a tiny electronic space, yet the values of such products and services far exceed the value of products and services in other sectors. Since they are valuable, organizations need to manage them in such a way as to develop and retain them and continue doing business with them. This is what this book is about: a study of talent management strategies and practices applied to digital talent by companies that aim to improve the attraction, development and retention of such digitally skilled and highly sought-after professionals and managers. This new kind of talent management, what this book refers to as human-centered 'digital talent management' (DTM), takes into account the distinctive nature of digital talent, which we argue is different in important ways from talent who performs and carries out digital roles, activities and tasks to a limited extent only.

The research presented in this book builds upon a research project, which ran throughout 2020, and was partly funded by NTT DATA Romania. This research project investigated talent management practices in national IT&C companies and subsidiaries of multinational companies located in Cluj-Napoca and other cities across Romania. Cluj-Napoca is one of the largest digital hubs in Romania, while Romania's IT&C industry constitutes one of the fastest growing digital ecosystems in the European Union. We expanded the research carried out during this project and collected additional data from nine companies, three of which are large (ranging from 400 to 950 employees), while six are small- and medium-sized (from a minimum of 20 to a maximum of 200 employees): two of them with Romanian ownership, while seven are Romania-based subsidiaries of multinational companies. As part of this research, we interviewed approximately 40 software developers, engineers and consultants with different digital expertise that includes methodological and technical development, Java, embedded systems, SAP, Application Management Outsourcing (AMO), user experience (UX) and user interface (UI). We also interviewed approximately 35 human resource and workforce management staff members, chief executive officers (CEOs) and management board members. In addition, we analyzed organizational reports concerning strategic development, talent management procedures, new joiners' and exit reports and talent satisfaction surveys. The timeframe of our research overlapped in part with the outbreak and worldwide spread of the global COVID-19 pandemic, as well as the policy responses to the latter. Some of the research was carried out before and some after the COVID-19 outbreak. This enabled us to explore the implications of the pandemic on digital talent management. Hereafter, we reflect on what we have found during this process.

We acknowledge that our work builds upon the shoulders of giants and that considerable research has been carried out in the fields of human resource management, talent management and organizational retention and turnover. We also acknowledge a growing body of research on the work life and practices of knowledge workers generally and software developers specifically. We recognize this existing work by pulling together insights from different streams of research and employing them in order to articulate the concept of digital talent and delineate organizational digital talent management strategies and practices. We hope that by drawing attention to the specific nature of digital talent and the implications thereof on digital talent management, our book will be of great interest to human resource management scholars and students, as well as CEOs and business/line managers working in partnership with human resource professionals to find the most effective way to attract, develop and retain digital talent. Last but not least, our book is of interest to higher education institutions who play a key role in shaping digital talent's abilities, competencies and skills, and to national, regional and local policy makers who increasingly work alongside companies to help them source digital talent across different industries and sectors.

We would like to thank our digital talent: the respondents and interviewees who have given us a moment of their time, which was particularly precious in pandemic times, to share their views and experience with us. We benefitted from the intellectual input of the research team at the University of Vaasa's Innovation and Entrepreneurship InnoLab, who, prior to the writing of this book, carried out the research project entitled 'Digitalisation Academy: Piloting and Creating a Nationwide Model to Tackle Talent Shortage and Improve Digital Competences', funded by Finland's Ministry of Employment and Economic Affairs. We are grateful to Hugh Scullion who offered guidance with regard to building the methodological design for the empirical research of this study. We would like to thank Adam Smale for his useful feedback on a previous draft and two anonymous Palgrave Macmillan reviewers for their helpful suggestions on the proposal of this book. Last but not least, a special thank you goes out to NTT DATA Romania for providing partial financial support to enable the completion of the research that led to the writing of this book.

We, the authors, represent both the world of research and the world of practice, which we believe adds value to this book and points to a fruitful interplay between academic scholarship and management experience in the IT&C industry. Considering the composition of our team and the content of this book, we hope that the words of this book may also speak to digital talent themselves who might be surprised to discover a little bit more about themselves as they go through the pages of this book.

Vaasa, Finland
Cluj-Napoca, Romania

Sorin Dan
Diana Ivana
Monica Zaharie
Daniel Metz
Mihaela Drăgan

Contents

About the Authors

Sorin Dan (PhD, KU Leuven) is a postdoctoral researcher at the University of Vaasa's Innovation and Entrepreneurship InnoLab, Finland. Dan's expertise includes talent management, innovation studies and administrative reform. His research has been published by Palgrave Macmillan and journals, such as *Public Management Review* and *Public Performance & Management Review.*

Diana Ivana (PhD, Babeş-Bolyai University) is a lecturer at Babeş-Bolyai University and an HR manager at NTT DATA Romania. Her work focuses on talent management, quality management and entrepreneurship. In both her research and teaching, Ivana has extensively drawn upon her experience in talent management in the IT&C industry.

Monica Zaharie (PhD, Babeş-Bolyai University) is an associate professor at Babeş-Bolyai University. Her expertise includes human resource management, talent management and international assignments. Zaharie has co-authored five books and her research has been published in international journals, such as *European Management Journal, Scientometrics* and *the Journal of Business Ethics.*

Daniel Metz (PhD, Babeş-Bolyai University) is Chairman of the Board of Directors at NTT DATA Romania and associate lecturer at Babeş-Bolyai University. Metz was previously the founder and CEO of EBS Romania, a company founded in 2000 and acquired by NTT DATA in 2013. He had previously held senior positions in a German company.

Mihaela Drăgan (PhD, Babeş-Bolyai University) is a professor and head of the Department of Economics and Business Administration in German language at Babeş-Bolyai University. Drăgan has authored 3 books in German, co-authored 5 other books and published over 80 articles in various national and international journals.

List of Figures

List of Tables

CHAPTER 1

Introduction

Abstract The introduction sets the scene of the entire book and provides an outline of each chapter. It argues that despite the development of a wide spectrum of digital activities and tasks, there is still considerable mystery related to the professionals and managers who perform these roles. This chapter introduces the concept of digital talent and shows that stereotypical portrayals of computer programmers are unlikely to reflect the manifold nature of digital talent. Considering digital talent's distinctive characteristics, the chapter calls for the need for a new kind of talent management, which we refer to as 'digital talent management' that is applicable to digital talent and decidedly integrates digital talent's distinctive characteristics into talent management strategies and practices in a human-centered manner.

Keywords Digital talent • Digital talent management (DTM) • Digital talent attraction • Digital talent development • Digital talent retention

The contribution to innovation and economic development of professionals and managers with digital abilities, competencies and skills is undisputable. A large share of present-day economic activity rests upon and is supported by computer programs and digital technologies that such professionals and their organizations design, develop and maintain (Balthasar et al., 2010; Niemi et al., 2021). A wide spectrum of new roles and tasks

S. Dan et al., *Digital Talent Management*,
https://doi.org/10.1007/978-3-030-76750-1_1

have surfaced over the years, and along with them, a variety of digital competencies have come to the fore worldwide. As a global 2019 survey on 26,806 digital experts from 180 countries has outlined, such digital competencies include but are not limited to (Boston Consulting Group, 2019, p. 2):

- Data mining, engineering and analytics;
- Programming and web development, including frontend and backend;
- Digital marketing, including influencer marketing and marketing analytics;
- Digital design, consisting of user experience (UX) and user interface (UI) design;
- Mobile application development;
- Artificial intelligence and machine learning;
- Agile ways of working;
- Robotics and automation engineering.

However, although the role of digital talent in the labor market and organizations has continued to grow, there is still considerable mystery related to the nature of digital talent, its relation to other types of talent and the implications for talent management. Stereotypical portrayals of 'computer geeks', such as the one shown in Fig. 1.1, who do nothing else but sit contained, focused and relaxed in front of a computer screen and type symbols, abound in the media.

Nevertheless, this simplified perception has started to be challenged by research on the nature of digital work and work practices of digital talent, which found that digital talent spends at least as much time on interacting and collaborating as on searching for information, reading documentation and writing code (Gonçalves et al., 2011; Marks & Scholarios, 2008; Meyer et al., 2017). Surrounded by their technical infrastructure, which they need to master well, digital talent tends to be perceived as knowledge workers *par excellence* who take a focused and planned, step-by-step approach to organizing and implementing their work. According to this 'rationalized' working method, there is limited room for personal creativity, which runs against the very notion of knowledge work, which is creative by definition (Barrett, 2005). Research on the work life of digital talent, however, has further shown that digital work is more fragmented than believed, and digital talent frequently switches between different

Fig. 1.1 Portrayal of a stereotypical computer programmer. (Source: Pixabay)

technical and interactive activities, both work and non-work related, influencing productivity and well-being (Meyer et al., 2017; Singer et al., 2010). The global COVID-19 pandemic has exacerbated these challenges by putting additional strain on digital talent and their families and children (Ralph et al., 2020).

This book argues that the interplay between the technical and social facets of digital work is a more accurate reflection of the reality of the current work life and practices of digital talent. This same interplay between 'the digital' and 'the human' lies at the core of this book's understanding of the notion of digital talent. It takes two to tango, and the digital side is as important to the human side as the human is to the digital one. Yet, there is a need for more research that integrates these two facets and provides a more holistic conceptualization of digital talent and uses it to analyze the practical implications of the specific nature of digital talent for talent attraction, development and retention. Figure 1.2 depicts this

Fig. 1.2 Symbolic representation of the interplay between the digital and human facets of digital talent. (Source: Pixabay)

interplay and symbolizes the ‘mystery’ that characterizes the notion of digital talent.

Considering that digital talent constitutes the engine of innovation and business development, they are particularly valuable to organizations (Balthasar et al., 2010). Companies develop talent management programs and practices that aim to increase job satisfaction and improve organizational commitment and retention (George, 2015). As this book shows, the specific characteristics of digital talent pose talent management challenges for organizations which need to ensure that one of their most valuable resources—highly mobile and educated staff with expert-level digital skills—decide to remain within the organization (Restubog et al., 2006). This is what this book sets out to explore: talent management strategies and practices applied to digital talent with the aim to attract, develop and retain them.

The central argument of this book is that both the shared and distinctive features of digital talent have managerial implications for talent management. We argue that the distinctive nature of digital talent calls for a renewed talent management, which we refer to as 'digital talent management' (DTM) that decidedly integrates such distinctive nature into organizational talent management strategies and practices in a human-centered way. To manage their digital talent, organizations need to know them well and understand their specific nature along with other distinctive, 'God-given' characteristics that make each person unique. On the basis of this knowledge, they need to adopt a development and retention-centered mindset. This involves acting across the different stages of the talent management cycle, from recruitment to onboarding and motivation, in such a way as to facilitate professional and personal development and make people want to stay. Our book seeks to contribute theoretically by developing the concept of digital talent and delineating the sphere of digital talent management based on existing research on talent management and information and communication technology (IT&C) professionals and empirical research carried out within IT&C companies and presented in this book. Our research aims to contribute to talent management practices by examining the implications of managing digital talent for improving their organizational attraction, development and retention. We carry out this research in a new context. This context includes a fast-growing digital innovation ecosystem that comprises a set of nine Romanian IT&C companies and subsidiaries of multinational companies and the global COVID-19 pandemic, which has significantly impacted organizational and personal work arrangements and practices (Ralph et al., 2020).

Chapter 2 lays out the foundation for the remaining chapters. It reviews the literature on digital work as performed by IT&C professionals and managers and the theoretical literature regarding talent management. The chapter provides an original conceptualization of digital talent that reflects digital talent's distinctive professional characteristics and personal human attributes. It shows that two interlinked facets: a digital and a human one best reflect the nature of digital talent and argues that a human-centered approach to understanding and managing digital talent is required that goes beyond the talent-as-object and talent-as-subject approaches found in the general talent management literature. This chapter then distinguishes between different groupings of digital talent depending on the range of actors and scope of activities considered, and ends with defining digital talent.

Starting from the characteristics of digital talent outlined in Chap. 2, Chap. 3 surveys the literature regarding organizational attraction, development and retention strategies as they apply to digital talent. Combined with the literature review, the chapter integrates key practices found in the IT&C industry globally and discusses their implications for digital talent management.

Chapter 4 constitutes the empirical chapter of this book. Building on the scholarly literature outlined in Chap. 3, it presents and analyzes original, empirical evidence on the effectiveness of digital talent management strategies and practices implemented by IT&C companies. Balancing the organizational and individual perspective, the chapter provides insights on effective digital talent management that aimed to attract, develop and retain digital talent. It does so using a qualitative research design that included individual interviews with representatives of the management board of IT&C companies, HR staff and IT&C professionals.

Chapter 5 concludes by bringing together the main arguments of the book and outlining their implications for research and practice. It shows the contribution that this book makes to the existing literature by developing the concept of digital talent and delineating digital talent management as a human-centered talent management process that consists of strategies and practices applicable to digital talent. The chapter outlines the managerial implications of this research by emphasizing how COVID-19 has impacted the management of digital talent. It ends with a look into the future of digital talent management in post-COVID-19 times—a future that is both uncertain and different from before, perhaps endlessly so.

References

Balthasar, A., Bättig, C., Thierstein, A., & Wilhelm, B. (2010). "Developers": Key Actors of the Innovation Process: Types of Developers and Their Contacts to Institutions Involved in Research and Development, Continuing Education and Training, and the Transfer of Technology. *Technovation, 20*, 523–538.

Barrett, R. (2005). The Reality of Software Developing. In R. Barrett (Ed.), *Management, Labour Process and Software Development: Reality Bites* (pp. 197–206). Routledge.

Boston Consulting Group. (2019). *Decoding Digital Talent, What 27,000 Digital Experts in 180 Countries Tell Us About Their Mobility and Work Preferences.* Boston Consulting Group & the Network.

George, C. (2015). Retaining Professional Workers: What Makes Them Stay? *Employee Relations, 37*(1), 102–121.

Gonçalves, M. K., de Souza, L. R., & Gonzalez, V. M. (2011). Collaboration, Information Seeking and Communication: An Observational Study of Software

Developers' Work Practices. *Journal of Universal Computational Science, 17*(14), 1913–1930.

Marks, A., & Scholarios, D. (2008). Choreographing a System: Skill and Employability in Software Work. *Economic and Industrial Democracy, 29*(1), 96–124.

Meyer, A., Barton, L. E., Fritz, T., Murphy, G. C., & Zimmermann, T. (2017). The Work Life of Developers: Activities, Switches and Perceived Productivity. *IEEE Transactions on Software Engineering, 43*(12), 1178–1193.

Niemi, M. K., Dan, S., Kalliokoski, J., Shahzad, K., Shakeel, S.R., Alagirisamy, R. & Laurila, I. (2021). *Talent Retention and the Development of Digital Skills: A study of the ecosystem-based Digitalisation Academy located in Vaasa, Finland.* Publications of the Ministry of Affairs and Employment 2021:23, Helsinki, http://urn.fi/URN:ISBN:978-952-327-840-0.

Ralph, P., Baltes, S., Adisaputri, G., Torkar, R., Kovalenko, V., Kalinowski, M., Novielli, N., Yoo, S., Devroey, X., Tan, X., Zhou, M., Turhan, B., Hoda, R., Hata, H., Robles, G., Fard, A. M., & Alkadhi, R. (2020). Pandemic Programming: How COVID-19 Affects Software Developers and How Their Organizations Can Help. *Empirical Software Engineering, 25*, 4927–4496.

Restubog, S. L. D., Bordia, P., & Tang, R. L. (2006). Effects of Psychological Contract Breach on Performance of IT Employees: The Mediating Role of Affective Commitment. *Journal of Occupational and Organizational Psychology, 79*, 299–306.

Singer, J., Lethbridge, T., Vinson, N., & Anquetil, N. (2010). An Examination of Software Engineering Work Practices. In *Proceedings CASCON 1st Decade High Impact Papers* (pp. 174–188).

CHAPTER 2

'Digital Talent'—A New Breed of Talent Calling for a New Kind of Talent Management

Abstract This chapter sets up the conceptual foundation for the remaining chapters, by reviewing the literature on digital work as performed by information and communication technology professionals and managers and the literature on talent management that focuses on defining talent. It then provides an original conceptualization of digital talent that reflects the latter's distinctive professional characteristics and unique personal attributes. It shows that two interlinked facets—a digital and a human one—best reflect the nature of digital talent and argues that a human-centered approach to conceptualizing and managing talent is required, going beyond the talent-as-object and talent-as-subject approaches found in the talent management literature. The chapter distinguishes between different groupings of digital talent depending on the range of actors and scope of activities considered, and ends with defining digital talent.

Keywords Digital talent • Definition • Digital facet • Human facet • Human-centered digital talent management

This chapter sets out to explore the specificity of digital talent and the implications of this specificity for digital talent management (DTM) within organizations. We use the term 'digital talent' to denote a wide spectrum of professionals and managers who possess digital abilities, competencies and skills and work in a growing number of industries and sectors

S. Dan et al., *Digital Talent Management*,
https://doi.org/10.1007/978-3-030-76750-1_2

worldwide. Digital talent occupies a central place in the current Fourth Industrial Revolution (Industry 4.0), characterized by increased automation and a spread and deepening of the trend toward the development and use of digital technologies. Digitalization itself, however, does not guarantee organizational success. In addition to the appropriate technical infrastructure, organizations need to have the right human resource capabilities to implement and benefit from digital technologies (Halme & Niinikoski, 2019). Digital talent helps create, run and develop a variety of innovative technologies that make a significant contribution to national, regional and local economies (Evangelista et al., 2014). Digital talent contributes to fostering business development across a variety of industries and sectors.

Faced with talent shortage and deteriorating socio-demographic trends, which are particularly severe in some regions, governments and industries are struggling to ensure adequate digital competencies and skills to maintain and foster growth. To address talent shortage, national governments, regions, cities and companies across the world have developed and implemented talent management practices to meet the growing need for a digitally skilled workforce (Rilla et al., 2018). Talent mobility and turnover, which are particularly high among highly skilled and specialized information and communication technology (IT&C) professionals, impact organizations' budgets and their development potential (Boston Consulting Group, 2019; Holtom et al., 2008). Since mismanagement of digital talent can be costly, it is important for organizations to adopt and systematically apply talent management principles that do not compromise mutually agreed arrangements and their psychological contract (Rousseau et al., 2018). Such contract breach can lead to loss of trust, poor satisfaction and commitment, which can result in digital talent's turnover (Flood et al., 2001; Muratbekova-Touron & Galindo, 2018; Scholarios et al., 2008). Therefore, from a managerial standpoint, knowing what makes digital talent tick, and what factors contribute to their satisfaction and organizational commitment, particularly in turbulent times, has the potential to improve talent development and retention.

Understanding Digital Talent

As a type of knowledge workers, digital talent is not entirely new. More than 60 years ago, Peter Drucker, in his 1959 book *Landmarks of Tomorrow*, reflected on the nature of knowledge workers. Years later, he drew again the attention to the pivotal role of knowledge work and its managerial implications by stating that "to make knowledge work productive will be the great management task of this century, just as to make manual work productive was the management task of the last century" (Age of Discontinuity, p. 290). Yet, the advent of the internet and increased digitalization and automation have added new layers and features to productive work while replacing some of the existing organizational arrangements, work methods and practices. These are specific to the digital environment in which digital talent is educated and trained and in which they exercise their profession and carry out their work on a daily basis. This digital environment and the nature of digital work are novel, although they are far from static and could best be described as a moving target. In the same way as Peter Drucker did years ago, we can affirm that making digital work productive and effective on a sustainable basis is one of the greatest challenges of present-day organizations, be they business, governmental or non-governmental organizations.

The performance and success of business organizations which operate in dynamic and competitive industries hinge on their ability to attract, develop and retain talented people (Niemi et al., 2021). However, although research on human resource and talent management is growing, and a sub-part of this research deals with the management and development of professionals in IT&C companies, there is relatively little academic research that connects talent management with the specific features of IT&C professionals and managers (Muratbekova-Touron & Galindo, 2018; Marks & Huzzard, 2008; Scholarios et al., 2008). A great deal of the existing work in this area consists of media and journalistic accounts and consultancy reports, which, although useful, are theory-free. As previous research has documented, and as we show in this volume, digital talent exhibits a set of characteristics that sets them apart from professionals and managers working in other professions and performing other roles and tasks. These features include digital talent's propensity for national and international mobility (Boston Consulting Group, 2019), identification with their employer versus their profession (Scholarios & Marks, 2004), their learning preferences and needs (Barrett, 2004; Dekas et al., 2013), and expectations related to work conditions (Muratbekova-Touron & Galindo, 2018). Such characteristics are not necessarily unique to digital talent and may be shared with professionals and managers who work in other knowledge-intensive professions (Davenport, 2005; Licorish & MacDonell, 2017). However, digital talent is also shaped by the digital nature of their roles and tasks and their work environment, which have distinctive features. These distinctive features contribute to the specificity of digital talent that distinguishes them from other knowledge workers, the same way teachers, surgeons or accountants, for example, constitute distinctive professional groups.

However, our concept of digital talent is not a one-dimensional, monolithic construct that does not allow for variation. While digital talent possesses a set of abilities, competencies and skills, both technical and social, and performs a set of roles, activities and tasks, the latter vary from one setting or person to another. Not all digital talent needs to have the same attributes and carry out the same activities, tasks and duties to perform well on the job. Research has documented this variety in the very nature of digital work, highlighting the growing importance of new sets of digital skills such as artificial intelligence (AI) and agile (Boston Consulting Group, 2019) and interpersonal abilities in addition to technical competencies (Marks & Scholarios, 2008). Our conceptualization of digital talent does not only capture the variation in the nature of digital work, but also reflects the individual and distinctive nature of each digital talent along with his/her preferences, needs, values, goals and work practices (Meyer et al., 2017; Ralph et al., 2020). This implies that while digital talent shares common characteristics and, at a general level, may be analyzed as a specific type of knowledge workers (as in the case of, e.g., high-school math teachers or pediatricians), there is also considerable variation between them.

In fleshing out the concept of digital talent, it is important to stress that the available evidence-based talent management academic literature on what digital talent represents is limited yet growing. This does not only concern the number of studies, but also the context in which studies are carried out and their conceptual development. Key concepts such as talent or digital are rarely defined in detail and in a systematic way (Gallardo-Gallardo et al., 2013). Both older studies (e.g., Barrett, 2004; Marks & Scholarios, 2008; Scholarios & Marks, 2004) and more recent ones (e.g., Licorish & MacDonell, 2017; Meyer et al., 2017; Muratbekova-Touron & Galindo, 2018) note that our understanding of who digital talent is and what digital talent does are influenced more by media news and context-specific practitioner stories than by rigorous academic research. This can be explained by the novelty of many of the current digital professions, their dynamic nature and the strong influence exercised by Silicon Valley hi-tech giants that set the pace globally when it comes to digital work. Yet, the extent to which the principles and practices that are common for these hi-tech companies are used by other smaller and less visible organizations across the world, which constitute the bulk of national, regional and local economies, remains an open question. Given the contextual determinism of effective talent management, there are reasons to believe that what works well in Silicon Valley may not work well elsewhere due to significant economic, social, cultural and managerial differences (Gallardo-Gallardo et al., 2020).

Moreover, there is further research on knowledge workers more generally than on digital talent specifically (Benson & Brown, 2007; Dekas et al., 2013; O'Donohue et al., 2007; Scarbrough, 1999). Knowledge workers include a variety of non-manufacturing, "intellectual" professionals who "think for a living" and have a "high degree of expertise, education or experience, and the primary purpose of their jobs involves the creation, distribution or application of knowledge" (Davenport, 2005, p. 10). However, while digital talent shares certain characteristics of knowledge workers, they are also part of a distinctive profession with its own principles, values and operating procedures. Digital talent is considered to have a high professional status; they are elite "gold-collar" experts who epitomize the very notion of knowledge work (Barrett, 2001). This status is known to be rewarded with commensurate work conditions, compensation and benefits, among which modern office space that inspires creativity, flexible work arrangements, competitive salary and benefits package that seek to attract, motivate and retain digital talent in-house. These rewards may be complemented by team-building sessions that hone digital talent's interpersonal and collaborative abilities and a variety of learning workshops that keep talent abreast of the latest technologies. As knowledge workers do, digital talent professionals and managers "think for a living" (Davenport, 2005), but they do so with different tools than other knowledge workers. They code for a living. They digitalize things for a living, and they do so for others to use in their daily work. They design and produce with their own minds and maintain the functionality of the digital infrastructure on which a great deal of economic and social activity rests nowadays. They possess a high degree of specific technical expertise, which, for non-experts and outsiders to the profession, can constitute a black box that is difficult to understand. Because of their expertise, some scholars call them 'archetypal knowledge workers' or 'symbolic analysts' who master information to create and fix digital products and services that have both a high economic and social value (Barrett, 2004).

Nevertheless, some scholars find that perceptions about digital talent's professional status are overrated and these perceptions fail to account for the variety of digital work, which does not include only knowledge creation, but also less elitist roles and tasks such as support activities, testing, quality control or maintenance (Kraft, 1999). This implies that digital talent's work may include characteristics of both service-based knowledge work and Taylorized industrial production (Marks & Scholarios, 2008). Activities such as the above, which are by no means insignificant, yet less visible and enjoying a different status compared to knowledge creation, may explain why digital talent can also have a less favorable popular perception. More specifically, digital talent may be associated with computer nerds and geeks who enjoy quiet time with their computer or software program rather than interpersonal relations (Marks & Huzzard, 2008). However, this view, negative though it may be, ignores the important role of focus and commitment to productive and creative digital work (Singer et al., 2010). It also fails to consider that one of the productivity challenges faced by digital talent is the increased work fragmentation due to planned meetings, e-mail use and irrelevant activities (Meyer et al., 2017). This association of digital talent with overly technical behavior has been challenged by the increased importance of generic, managerial and interactive skills to digital talent's dynamic work. Existing research into digital work practices suggests that digital talent spends considerable time working in teams, collaborating with colleagues, interacting at various workshops and conferences and online forums to exchange information and learn from peers (Licorish & MacDonell, 2017; Ralph et al., 2020). These social competencies are complementary, rather than antithetical, to technical expertise (Marks & Scholarios, 2008). This implies that the type of work performed by digital talent professionals and managers and their particularly close connection with computer software does not nullify the importance of interpersonal skills for effective digital work.

Another distinctive feature of digital talent concerns their high propensity toward learning (Meyer et al., 2017). The changing nature of digital work and constant technological development emphasize that learning is a prerequisite to job performance. This explanation is external to digital talent. However, some scholars, particularly those who underline the knowledge-intensive dimension of digital work, suggest that digital talent learns not necessarily because they are required to, but because they so desire (Fang & Neufeld, 2009). According to this explanation, they thrive as they learn more, and thus, the availability of learning opportunities becomes an important requirement for the digital talent's job satisfaction, development and organizational commitment.

Research also notes the distinctiveness of digital talent's professional autonomy, identity and mobility patterns, and the way in which these values and preferences influence organizational attraction, development and retention. Digital talent is believed to enjoy a high degree of autonomy both at a personal level and as a profession. At a personal level, some scholars suggest that digital talent prefers to be given the freedom to organize and carry out their work within a broad framework, as mutually agreed with the organization, rather than to be managed closely (Barrett, 2004). As part of a profession, with its own distinctive features, digital talent favors an increased role in regulating their own profession and channeling its development (Muratbekova-Touron & Galindo, 2018). As in the case of other professions, this may be explained by the belief that the rules of the game are best managed by those who know them best. The highly technical nature of digital trends, which may be difficult for outsiders to comprehend, may warrant this approach. The important economic impact of knowledge-intensive industries and their strong bargaining power has policy, as well as organizational and individual implications. Research suggests that digital talent identifies themselves more with their profession and set of competencies than with a specific organization (Scholarios & Marks, 2004). Their favorable labor market position means that digital talent can change employers more easily than the professionals and managers who do not possess expert-level digital competencies and skills.

Evidence on digital talent's mobility preferences indicate that talent with expert-level digital skills is more likely to move to another country than non-experts (Boston Consulting Group, 2019). This same research found that more than two-thirds of the surveyed expert-level digital talent and, in some countries, 70% are willing to move compared with 50% of professionals who do not possess expert-level digital skills. This has important managerial implications as organizations need to strive to retain their most valuable talent. For this reason, companies, such as well-known hi-tech giants, seek to instill a sense of organizational identity and belonging to create emotional and psychological bonds that strengthen commitment to the organization and improve retention (Ortlieb & Sieben, 2012). This can range from corporate social responsibility actions to audacious mission statements, which controversial though they may be (see, to name just an example, Shoshana Zuboff's treatment of surveillance capitalism), act as a magnet for digital talent. Highly visible examples include Facebook's mission, that is, "to give people the power to build community and bring the world closer together" or Google's "to organize the world's information and make it universally accessible and useful". Yet, the implementation and effectiveness of such approaches in other organizational, cultural and socio-economic contexts, beyond the glamorous Silicon Valley, may be more limited (Gallardo-Gallardo et al., 2020).

Moreover, digital talent does not form a uniform group of professionals. Although they work across multiple inter-related industries, possess complementary digital skills and perform related roles and tasks, there is considerable variety between these industries, skills, roles and tasks. It is clear by now, based on our theoretical discussion, that not all digital talent is the same, and a conceptualization of digital talent needs to capture this variety. There are common, general trends concerning their socio-demographic data, preferences and values, but also significant variety depending on national, regional, cultural and individual factors. Digital talent has different work habits and productivity patterns: some are morning persons, others are low-at-lunch, whereas others are afternoon people, and these habits tend to be personal (Meyer et al., 2017). Moreover, digital talent responds differently to crises and conflict. Research on digital talent's work practices and well-being during the COVID-19 pandemic found that (Ralph et al., 2020):

- The pandemic has had a negative effect on well-being and productivity and the two concepts are inter-related;
- Disaster preparedness, fear induced by the pandemic and home office arrangements impact the well-being and productivity;
- Parents, women and digital talent with disabilities may be disproportionally affected;
- Digital talent's needs are different and require tailored support.

Other documented characteristics of digital talent include (Boston Consulting Group, 2019):

- Although digital talent has a higher propensity to move internationally for career development than talent without digital skills, this propensity significantly depends on the state of the economy in the country of origin, availability of career opportunities abroad, as well as language, cultural and other personal preferences;
- Most digital talent do not hold middle or senior management positions: only 9% own a company or work in senior management, 21%

work in middle management, whereas 29% work in lower management and 41% have no managerial responsibilities;

- Contrary to popular perceptions, digital talent's preferred employer is not start-ups, but large companies, followed by self-employed arrangements, small or medium-sized enterprises and start-ups;
- Digital talent's top five skills include, in this order: data mining, programming and web development, mobile application development, digital marketing and digital design (user experience and user interface);
- Digital talent is educated and trained, yet few have a doctorate: 38% have a bachelor's degree and 38% a master's degree, while only 4% of respondents have earned a doctorate;
- Most digital talent professionals are male: close to 70% compared to 30% who are female;
- The top six factors valued the most on the job by digital talent consist of, in this order: good work-life balance, learning and training opportunities, career development prospects, good relationship with colleagues, financial compensation and good relationship with manager.

Table 2.1 brings together key characteristics of digital talent.

Defining Digital Talent

To position our concept of digital talent into the organizational talent management literature, we will first review below certain conceptual issues related to the concept of talent as found in this literature. Then, we propose a human-centered conceptualization of digital talent and show in what ways this conceptualization differs from existing approaches. Following this, we define digital talent according to the range of actors and scope of activities that are included in digitalization processes.

In everyday language, talent refers to a special skill or ability, or to someone who has an above-average education, or who has achieved a high level of performance in a specific activity such as sports or arts. Research on talent management has been growing since the publication of the seminal 1998 McKinsey's report on the 'War for Talent'. Despite this research and the frequent use of the word talent in both practice and research, there is considerable ambiguity concerning the meaning of the concept of talent (Gallardo-Gallardo & Thunnissen, 2016). Talent is rarely defined explicitly, and its meaning is influenced by implicit and subjective

Table 2.1 Providing the contours of digital talent

Characteristic of digital talent	*Description*	*Reference*
Socio-demographics	Predominantly male, yet a rising share of female talent	Boston Consulting Group (2019)
Education	Well-educated, but not exclusively highly educated: at least a college degree for the majority, yet 20% without a college degree and 4% with a doctorate	Boston Consulting Group (2019), Marks and Scholarios (2008)
Expertise	High level of digital expertise, acquired through formal education and/or constant training and learning	Muratbekova-Touron and Galindo (2018)
Social status	High social status: gold-collar experts, knowledge workers who think for a living; archetypal knowledge workers; yet also perceived to have negative computer-nerd traits and poor interpersonal skills; they might perform more mechanical, repetitive and less knowledge-intensive tasks	Barrett (2001, 2004), Davenport (2005), Kraft (1999), Marks and Huzzard (2008)
Work conditions	Above labor market averages, modern office spaces, flexible work arrangements, competitive salary and benefits package based on performance	Muratbekova-Touron and Galindo (2018)
Performance orientation	Above-average achievement goals and targets, preoccupied with fixing and making things work	Meyer et al. (2017), Ralph et al. (2020)
Professional identity	Identify well with the profession, industry or set of skills and a preference for autonomy	Barrett (2004), Scholarios and Marks (2004)
Competencies and skills	A variety of technical, digital, and IT&C skills coupled with a growing importance of general, transferable and social skills	Balthasar et al. (2010), Boston Consulting Group (2019), Marks and Scholarios (2008)
Learning orientation	High learning orientation determined by digital trends and digital talent's own learning orientation	Dekas et al. (2013), Fang and Neufeld (2009)
Employer preferences	Large companies followed by self-employed, small and medium-sized companies, start-ups and freelance work	Boston Consulting Group (2019)

(*continued*)

Table 2.1 (continued)

Characteristic of digital talent	*Description*	*Reference*
Management responsibilities	A good share of digital talent has no management responsibilities or work in lower management; only one tenth is represented by owners of companies or work in senior management	Boston Consulting Group (2019)
Work environment	Close connection to the digital field, by designing, creating or maintaining digital products and services	Gonçalves et al. (2011), Singer et al. (2010)
Work habits	Morning, low-at-lunch, and afternoon digital talent	Meyer et al. (2017)
Work practices	Increasingly fragmented and include a variety of activities: technical development, communication and interaction, searching for information and documentation	Gonçalves et al. (2011), Meyer et al. (2017), Singer et al. (2010), Licorish and MacDonell (2017), Marks and Scholarios (2008)
Productivity patterns	Positively influenced by user input and negatively by e-mail communication, meetings and other interruptions	Meyer et al. (2017)
Mobility patterns	More mobile than other talent workers, yet mobility patterns depend on the country of origin, career opportunities, language and cultural preferences	Boston Consulting Group (2019)
Job satisfaction and well-being	Influenced, in this order, by good work-life balance, learning opportunities, career development prospects, good work relationships and financial compensation	Boston Consulting Group (2019), Tripp et al. (2016), Ralph et al. (2020)
Organizational commitment	Less strong than in other less dynamic industries, yet it depends on the organizations' talent management strategy	Flood et al. (2001), Scholarios and Marks (2004)
Psychological contract	Balanced psychological contract that includes transactional, relational and ideological elements	Collins and Kehoe (2017), Muratbekova-Touron and Galindo (2018), Restubog et al. (2006)

Source: Authors' compilation

understandings of what talent represents (Tansley, 2011). There are two main conceptual approaches to talent in the academic literature: the object approach and the subject approach (Gallardo-Gallardo et al., 2013). The object approach sees talent as a set of characteristics of people, while the subject approach views talent as people. According to Gallardo-Gallardo et al., the former focuses on the skills and abilities, both inborn and acquired, that employees have, and the latter on talent as people. Four main complementary characteristics of talent as object are outlined: natural, inborn ability, mastery over a specific subject or field, commitment to an organization and fit within a certain organizational setting. In terms of talent as subject, there are two approaches depending on the breadth of coverage. The exclusive approach sees talent as an elite subset of the workforce (e.g., 5% or 10%) who either are high performers or hold a high level of potential (high potentials) to contribute to organizational objectives. By contrast, the inclusive approach views talent as all employees of an organization (Gallardo-Gallardo et al., 2013, p. 297).

The literature follows one or more of these different understandings, although usually only implicitly. Some scholars, however, spell out what they mean by talent. Some see talent as those "persons who have the potential to provide competitive advantage for a company" (Bethke-Langenegger et al., 2011, p. 527). For others, talent consists of "individuals with key technical and professional skills that are valuable advantages for firms competing in global markets" (Shin et al., 2019). Some scholars who follow the talent-as-object perspective define talent as "the sum of a person's abilities—his or her intrinsic gifts, skills, knowledge, experience, intelligence, judgement, attitude, character and drive. It also includes his or her ability to learn and grow" (Michaels et al., 2001, p. xii). A different definition views talent as "a person's recurring patterns of thought, feeling or behavior that can be productively applied" (Buckingham & Vosburgh, 2001, p. 21).

Following one approach to talent or another has a series of practical implications for human resource management. Leaders need to make decisions about whether it is desirable to invest in a few employees or in the entire workforce to achieve organizational success. Another implication deals with the assessment and inclusion of employees within talent pools and the measures and criteria that managers should use for this assessment. Critics of the exclusive approach warn of problems in evaluating the talent-spotting process objectively (Gallardo-Gallardo et al., 2013). In the worst-case scenario, this approach may lead to lifting a few employees up while putting most of the workforce down, which can lead to demotivation and turnover. The inclusive approach, however, may run contrary to the etymological and historical definition of talent, according to which talent is exclusive by definition. Moreover, an inclusive talent management approach may not be efficient to apply in practice, despite its desirable appeal (Collings & Mellahi, 2009; Lin, 2006).

We find Gallardo-Gallardo and colleagues' differentiations useful: talent as object identifies characteristics of people (i.e., what people have) while talent as subject reflects how individuals perform their job (i.e., what people do). Delineating each approach further into sub-components is equally useful. However, we see the importance of capturing the interplay between these two main approaches as well as the need to not only emphasize what professionals have and what they do, but also who and how they are. Who employees and managers are and how they are as distinctive human beings are relevant aspects that are missing from the available conceptualization. We argue that this is particularly important in the context of digital talent, which is a specific 'species' of talent, as outlined earlier in this chapter, and the digital dimension adds additional layers and features, which can lead to misspecification and ambiguity if it is not clearly defined.

This volume's conceptualization of digital talent is based on the empirical observation that digital talent embodies professionals and managers who work in a wide spectrum of professions and industries across the world. They are people with more or less similar abilities, competencies and skills, both technical and social, and who master these skills in different ways. They work in different organizational contexts, from large, multinational companies to small, freelance projects. In defining talent as people, we follow the subject approach. However, the subject approach is complemented by the object approach in such a way that we also delineate the range of abilities, competencies and skills, both innate and acquired, technical and interpersonal, which digital talent possesses and further develops on the job. Moreover, we argue for the need to account for each digital talent's distinctive, 'God-given' individual attributes and needs and incorporate this perspective into the existing approaches to defining and managing talent. Therefore, our understanding of digital talent recognizes that there are two closely interlinked facets to digital talent: a digital facet and a human one. The digital facet reflects the distinctly digital nature of IT&C work and includes characteristics related to abilities, competencies, and skills, but also to the work environment and the industries in which digital talent operates. The human facet of digital talent draws attention to each person's distinctive features, not as a skilled expert in, for example, machine learning, but on who and how that person is. This perspective is reflected in the human resource management literature that acknowledges the centrality of 'human' in human resource management (e.g., Winstanley & Woodall, 2000; Lepeley et al., 2021). We argue that such a human-centered approach goes beyond the existing subject and object approaches, and is particularly needed, although not exclusively, in the increasingly automated digital environments in which digital talent works. In these environments, it is, and will increasingly be, easy to lose sight of the fundamental role of human agency which should determine and control the process and outcomes of technological development.

Considering this discussion, in our view, digital talent can be defined in different ways depending on the range of actors that are included in digitalization processes and the scope of their activities. A standard definition of digitalization involves a transformation of analog data and information into a digital form. Digitalization also refers, however, to a replacement of the analog-type support used in administrative and economic activities with individual, group or social interactions that are carried out digitally. In this way, these activities acquire a digital character while the replacement process itself can be characterized as a process of digital transformation. In a broad sense, we distinguish between three main types of actors who contribute to digital transformation processes and who can be treated as digital talent by virtue of this contribution:

- First, digital talent includes the decision maker who sees an opportunity and acts upon it, to replace the analog support with a digital format. This may be the owner of the innovative idea concerning how analog data can be transformed into digital data (e.g., an inventor) or the leader of a social or economic entity who decides on the implementation of a digital transformation process in that entity (e.g., a manager of an organization);
- Second, digital talent incorporates the project manager who brings the innovative idea from the stage of invention to the stage of a marketable product or service. This second grouping also includes a process analyst, who, after evaluating existing organizational processes, designs the architecture of the new digital dimension; and
- Third, in a narrower sense, digital talent includes the technical implementers of the digital solution. These include software and hardware engineers who create a digital product, solution architects, software

Table 2.2 Three groupings of digital talent

Range of activities	*Range of actors*
Digital transformation decision-making	Owner of innovative idea
	Leader of social/economic entity/activity
Digital transformation process management	Project manager
	Process analyst
Digital transformation technical implementation and communication	Hardware and software engineers
	Solution architects
	Business consultants
	Software developers and testers
	Support engineers
	Big data and AI experts
	Digital marketing and social media specialists

Source: Authors' own

developers and testers, but also business consultants who parameterize digital solutions and train the staff involved in digitalization processes. This type of digital talent also includes specialists in digital marketing, social media, big data and AI who manage digitalization activities at an operational level and communicates their development and results internally and externally.

Table 2.2 provides examples of digital talent that take into account the three groupings outlined above, depending on digital talent's participation in digital transformation processes.

This overview is indicative only, not exhaustive, and it shows the wide spectrum of professionals, managers and leaders who operate in and contribute to digital transformation. They are all digital talent in this broad sense. However, much of the current academic literature deals with digital talent in a narrow sense and refers predominantly to our third group mentioned above, yet it is important not to lose sight of the larger array of people who shape digitalization processes and contribute, in different yet important ways, to digital transformation. It is important to underline that these actors and roles are not restricted to the IT&C industry, essential though this specific industry may be, since digital transformation cuts across multiple industries and sectors, all of which require the attraction, development and retention of digital talent. This is particularly relevant considering that digitalization is blurring industry boundaries and the mix of abilities, competencies and skills that are required. Effective digital talent management is thus a common denominator that pulls together organizations operating across different industries and sectors.

Considering this proposed classification, *we define digital talent as individuals who contribute to digitalization and digital transformation processes, regardless of their organizational form and structure, across different industries and sectors in one or more of the following ways: inventing/creating an idea that may subsequently become a new digital product/service; contributing, within a specific organizational setting, to one or more stages of the new digital product/service development process from concept/ideation to manufacture/launch and improvement; or leading an entity or activity, regardless of its organizational features, through which one or more of these roles, activities and tasks are carried out.*

On the basis of the empirical research presented in this book, and building on this first definition, we inductively developed a working definition of digital talent. This definition closely follows the seven stages of a new product development (NPD) process (e.g., Trott, 2016), which include concept/ideation; feasibility study and design planning; design and implement; testing and verification; validation and collateral production; manufacture/launch; and improvement. This definition follows a more specific set of actors than outlined above who operate within an organizational setting within the IT&C industry itself, whereas the previous definition reflects digital talent who operates across different industries and organizational forms. According to this level of analysis, *we define digital talent as individuals who: possess and productively employ, to different degrees, a variety of innate and/or acquired digital abilities, competencies and skills; operate within an organizational setting within the IT&C industry; and are responsible for activities, roles and tasks that cover one or more stages of a new product development process.* In view of this working definition, we distinguish between digital architects and designers who generate the concept and design of the digital product/service; project managers who are responsible for project planning; business analysts and consultants who carry out the analysis throughout a new product development process, both before and after manufacture/launch; and technical implementers who implement the technical solution. Technical implementation may involve coding, performed by developers; testing, carried out by testers; and support/maintenance, which is the responsibility of support engineers who may carry these tasks on a daily basis during implementation. Digital talent may employ different project approaches, such as linear sequential methodologies or agile technologies that are incremental and iterative.

References

Balthasar, A., Bättig, C., Thierstein, A., & Wilhelm, B. (2010). "Developers": Key Actors of the Innovation Process: Types of Developers and Their Contacts to Institutions Involved in Research and Development, Continuing Education and Training, and the Transfer of Technology. *Technovation, 20*, 523–538.

Barrett, R. (2001). Labouring Under an Illusion? The Labour Process of Software Development in the Australian Information Industry. *New Technology Work and Employment, 16*, 18–34.

Barrett, R. (2004). Working at Webboyz: An Analysis of Control Over the Software Development Labour. *Sociology, 38*(4), 777–794.

Benson, J., & Brown, M. (2007). Knowledge Workers, What Keeps Them Committed, What Turns Them Away. *Work, Employment and Society, 21*(1), 121–141.

Bethke-Langenegger, P., Mahler, P., & Staffelbach, B. (2011). Effectiveness of Talent Management Strategies. *European Journal of International Management, 5*(5), 524–539.

Boston Consulting Group. (2019). *Decoding Digital Talent, What 27,000 Digital Experts in 180 Countries Tell Us About Their Mobility and Work Preferences.* Boston Consulting Group & the Network.

Buckingham, M., & Vosburgh, R. M. (2001). The 21st Century Human Resources Function: It's the Talent, Stupid! *Human Resource Planning, 24*(4), 17–23.

Collings, D. G., & Mellahi, K. (2009). Strategic Talent Management: A review and research agenda. *Human Resource Management Review, 19*(4), 304–313.

Collins, C., & Kehoe, R. (2017). Examining Strategic Fit and Misfit in the Management of Knowledge Workers. *Industrial and Labor Relations Review, 70*(2), 308–335.

Davenport, T. H. (2005). *Thinking for a Living: How to Get Better Performances and Results from Knowledge Workers.* Harvard Business School Press.

Dekas, K. H., Bauer, T. N., & Welle, B. (2013). Organizational Citizenship Behavior, Version 2.0: A Review and Qualitative Investigation of OCBs for Knowledge Workers at Google and Beyond. *Academy of Management Perspectives, 27*(3), 219–237.

Evangelista, R., Guerrieri, P., & Meliciani, V. (2014). The Economic Impact of Digital Technologies in Europe. *Economics of Innovation and New Technology, 23*(8), 802–824.

Fang, Y., & Neufeld, D. (2009). Understanding Sustained Participation in Open Source Software Projects. *Journal of Management Information Systems, 25*(4), 9–50.

Flood, P., Turner, T., Ramamoorthy, N., & Pearson, J. (2001). Causes and Consequences of Psychological Contracts Among Knowledge Workers in the

High Technology and Financial Services Industries. *International Journal of Human Resource Management, 12*(7), 1152–1165.

Gallardo-Gallardo, E., & Thunnissen, M. (2016). Standing on the Shoulders of Giants? A Critical Review of Empirical Talent Management Research. *Employee Relations, 38*(1), 31–56.

Gallardo-Gallardo, E., Dries, N., & Gonzales-Cruz, T. F. (2013). What Is the Meaning of 'Talent' in the World of Work? *Human Resource Management Review, 23*, 290–300.

Gallardo-Gallardo, E., Thunnissen, M., & Scullion, H. (2020). Talent Management: Context Matters. *The International Journal of Human Resource Management, 31*(4), 457–473.

Gonçalves, M. K., de Souza, L. R., & Gonzalez, V. M. (2011). Collaboration, Information Seeking and Communication: An Observational Study of Software Developers' Work Practices. *Journal of Universal Computational Science, 17*(14), 1913–1930.

Halme, K., & Niinikoski, M.-L.. (2019). *Innovation Policy to Renew the Economy and Society.* Publications of the Ministry of Economic Affairs and Employment, 2019:7, Government of Finland.

Holtom, B. C., Mitchell, T. R., Lee, T. W., & Eberly, M. B. (2008). Turnover and Retention Research: a Glance at the Past, a Closer Review of the Present and a Venture into the Future. *The Academy of Management Annals, 2*(1), 231–274.

Kraft, P. (1999). To Control and Inspire: US Management in the Age of Computer Information Systems and Global Production. In M. Wardell, T. Steiger, & P. Meiksins (Eds.), *Rethinking the Labor Process* (pp. 17–36). State University of New York Press.

Lepeley, M. T., Morales, O., Essens, P., Beutell, N. J., & Majluf, N. (Eds.). (2021). *Human Centered Organizational Culture: Global Dimensions.* Routledge.

Licorish, S. A., & MacDonell, S. G. (2017). Exploring Software Developers' Work Practices: Task Differences, Participation, Engagement, and Speed of Task Resolution. *Information & Management, 54*(3), 364–382.

Lin, W. Z. (2006). The New Key Word 'Talent Management' in Retaining the Top Employees. *Human Capital Magazine.*

Marks, A., & Huzzard, T. (2008). Creativity and Workplace Attractiveness in Professional Employment. *Journal of Human Resource Costing & Accounting, 12*(3), 225–239.

Marks, A., & Scholarios, D. (2008). Choreographing A System: Skill and Employability in Software Work. *Economic and Industrial Democracy, 29*(1), 96–124.

Meyer, A., Barton, L. E., Fritz, T., Murphy, G. C., & Zimmermann, T. (2017). The Work Life of Developers: Activities, Switches and Perceived Productivity. *IEEE Transactions on Software Engineering, 43*(12), 1178–1193.

Michaels, E., Handfield-Jones, H., & Axelrod, B. (2001). *The War for Talent.* Harvard Business School Press.

Muratbekova-Touron, M., & Galindo, G. (2018). Leveraging Psychological Contracts as an HR Strategy: The Case of Software Developers. *European Management Journal, 36*, 717–726.

Niemi, M. K., Dan, S., Kalliokoski, J., Shahzad, K., Shakeel, S.R., Alagirisamy, R. & Laurila, I. (2021). *Talent Retention and the Development of Digital Skills: A study of the ecosystem-based Digitalisation Academy located in Vaasa, Finland.* Publications of the Ministry of Affairs and Employment 2021:23, Helsinki, http://urn.fi/URN:ISBN:978-952-327-840-0.

O'Donohue, W., Sheehan, C., Hecker, R., & Holland, P. (2007). The Psychological Contract of Knowledge Workers. *Journal of Knowledge Management, 11*(2), 73–82.

Ortlieb, R., & Sieben, B. (2012). How to Safeguard Critical Resources of Professional and Managerial Staff: Exploration of a Taxonomy of Resource Retention Strategies. *International Journal of Human Resource Management, 23*(8), 1688–1704.

Ralph, P., Baltes, S., Adisaputri, G., Torkar, R., Kovalenko, V., Kalinowski, M., Novielli, N., Yoo, S., Devroey, X., Tan, X., Zhou, M., Turhan, B., Hoda, R., Hata, H., Robles, G., Fard, A. M., & Alkadhi, R. (2020). Pandemic Programming: How COVID-19 Affects Software Developers and How Their Organizations Can Help. *Empirical Software Engineering, 25*, 4927–4496.

Restubog, S. L. D., Bordia, P., & Tang, R. L. (2006). Effects of Psychological Contract Breach on Performance of IT Employees: The Mediating Role of Affective Commitment. *Journal of Occupational and Organizational Psychology, 79*, 299–306.

Rilla, N., Deschryvere, M., Oksanen, J., Raunio, M., & van der Have, R. (2018). *Immigrants in the Innovation Economy: Lessons from Austria, Canada, Denmark and the Netherlands.* Publications of the Government's Analysis, Assessment and Research Activities 1/2018, Government of Finland, Prime Minister's Office.

Rousseau, D., Hansen, S., & Tomprou, M. (2018). A Dynamic Phase Model of Psychological Contract Processes. *Journal of Organizational Behaviour, 39*(9), 1081–1098.

Scarbrough, H. (1999). Knowledge as Work: Conflicts in the Management of Knowledge Workers. *Technology Analysis & Strategic Management, 11*(1), 5–16.

Scholarios, D., Van der Heijden, B. I. J. M., Van der Schoot, E., Bozionelos, N., Epitropaki, O., Jedrzejowicz, P., Knauth, P., Marzec, I., Mikkelsen, A., & van der Heijde, C. M. (2008). Employability and the Psychological Contract in European ICT Sector SMEs. *The International Journal of Human Resource Management, 19*, 1035–1055.

Scholarios, D. M., & Marks, A. (2004). Work-Life Balance and the Software Worker. *Human Resource Management Journal, 14*(2), 54–74.

Shin, G., Choi, J. N., & Moon, R. J. (2019). Skilled Migrants as Human and Social Capital in Korea. *Asian Survey, 59*(4), 673–692.

Singer, J., Lethbridge, T., Vinson, N., & Anquetil, N. (2010). An Examination of Software Engineering Work Practices. In *Proceedings CASCON 1st Decade High Impact Papers* (pp. 174–188).

Tansley, C. (2011). What Do We Mean By the Term 'Talent' in Talent Management? *Industrial and Commercial Training, 43*(5), 266–274.

Tripp, J. F., Riemenschneider, C., & Thatcher, J. B. (2016). Job Satisfaction in Agile Development Teams: Agile Development as Work Redesign. *Journal of the Association for Information Systems, 17*(4), 267–307.

Trott, P. (2016). *Innovation Management and New Product Development* (6th ed.). Pearson.

Winstanley, D., & Woodall, J. (2000). Towards a Human Centered Organisation. *Business & Professional Ethics Journal, 19*(3/4), 3–12.

CHAPTER 3

Digital Talent Management Strategies and Practices

Abstract This chapter surveys the literature regarding organizational attraction, development and retention strategies as they apply to digital talent. In combination with the literature review, the chapter integrates key practices found in the information and communication technology industry and discusses their implications for digital talent management.

Keywords Digital talent management (DTM) • Digital talent attraction • Digital talent development • Digital talent retention

Innovative, value-adding industries are vital to every country's economic growth, which hinges on ensuring smooth operations, with as few obstacles as possible, in order to achieve long-term development (Alias et al., 2016). A constant availability of a large pool of talented and experienced professionals and managers is crucial in order to achieve these goals. Over the recent decades, the information and communication technology (IT&C) industry has developed significantly, maintaining a steady growth especially in high-growth regions. This innovative industry has created a large number of high-paying and knowledge-based jobs, which fueled an increasing need for digital talent. An increased competition for specific IT&C competencies and skills created pressure for companies to increase wages and to invest in educational programs in order to develop the needed talent pool (Flecker, 2018). Informally nicknamed 'Silicon Valleys',

S. Dan et al., *Digital Talent Management*,
https://doi.org/10.1007/978-3-030-76750-1_3

various regions stepped in as technological hubs by creating a valuable pool of digital talent. Dealing with challenges regarding increased competition for performing digital roles and tasks, the pressure to increase wages and, more recently, a rapidly changing environment due to COVID-19, the IT&C industry worldwide is facing a significant transformation. This transformation calls for the need to adjust and/or reinvent existing talent management strategies and practices within each company in order to improve the organizational attraction, development and retention of digital talent, which has distinctive characteristics compared with talent who does not perform digital activities, roles and tasks.

But how could organizations reinvent talent management, and what specific digital talent management (DTM) strategies and practices may be effective at attracting, developing and retaining digital talent? Rapidly changing demographics, technological developments and increased globalization have a significant impact on the world of work (Halme & Niinikoski, 2019). This new context is disrupting human resource management and established practices may no longer meet the needs of talented employees and managers. As a result, organizations across sectors and industries have become increasingly interested in finding ways to develop a meaningful and rewarding talent experience that attracts, nurtures and retains talent (Claus, 2019). COVID-19, despite its considerable socio-economic impact, may not have significantly changed the fact that digital talent is highly sought after on the labor market worldwide and that millennials are searching for meaningfulness (Etzold et al., 2020). More than ever, there is a need for a supply of qualified professionals and managers that grows as industries and markets grow. New economic realities and competitive pressures require organizations to create a system for attracting and developing digital talent that is centered on medium and long-term digital talent retention (Barinova et al., 2020).

Software is 'eating the world' and its design, development and maintenance require highly qualified digital talent who possesses different skills and operates across multiple functional areas, such as database development, security, user interface (UI), mobile development, artificial intelligence (AI) and agile technologies (Boston Consulting Group, 2019; Montandon et al., 2021). These roles and tasks are not unique to the IT&C industry and cut across different industries that currently undergo digital transformation processes that require digital abilities and skills. As a result, there is a high demand for knowledge and expertise on how companies perform digital talent management that aims to ensure that such required digital abilities and skills are adequately and effectively employed. Considering the high international competition for digital talent, companies are not only looking at attracting the best performers externally, but also, importantly, they look within their own premises at developing and retaining their best performers (Rodrigues & Naidoo, 2016). The application of talent management practices can indicate an organization's commitment to manage human resources sustainably, possibly resulting in greater talent engagement, higher job satisfaction and lower turnover rates (Corporate Leadership Council, 2004). Organizational talent management could be defined as "a set of sustainable organizational strategies that use human capital to the competitive advantage of the organization, as well as a portfolio of integrated HR activities that result in putting the right people with the right competencies in the right job in the right place, and at the right cost" (Claus, 2019, p. 208).

Considering both organizational and individual factors that impact digital talent management, in what follows this chapter surveys and connects organizational retention strategies and practices with the other main functions of digital talent management: digital talent attraction and digital talent development, respectively.

Digital Talent Attraction

The first station of the 'organizational talent management itinerary' is digital talent attraction, which is presented by means of the following central functions: digital talent recruitment and selection and digital talent induction and onboarding. Recruitment plays an essential role considering that companies may need to search externally to employ talent who possesses IT&C knowledge and expertise in order to digitalize their products, services and processes (Gilch & Sieweke, 2020). Talent planning underlies talent recruitment, which needs to be aligned with digital talent's strategic objectives (Xu et al., 2017). The recruitment of digital talent takes different forms, and increasingly organizations have resorted to setting up close partnerships with technical institutes and universities and organizing internship programs leading to long-term recruitment (Niculescu et al., 2019).

In recruiting digital talent, building a strong and attractive employer branding and offering a compelling digital talent value proposition can provide strategic leverage for organizations that improves digital talent attraction regionally, nationally and internationally (Sparrow & Makram,

2015; Tikhonov, 2019). The development of a positive employer brand and a compelling digital talent value proposition can thus contribute to addressing the increased shortage of talent. This approach can improve talent attraction by allowing prospective candidates to favorably answer the question: "Why should I work in this company?" These strategies involve making a realistic and genuine promise that is attractive in the eyes of relevant talent (Trost, 2020). For example, in a recent empirical study of Russian IT&C companies, Tikhonov (2019) found that when selecting a job, applicants appreciate most the following talent management practices: compensation level; professional development/career; attractiveness of the task/project; team professionalism; and the possibility to work together with high-class specialists. Employers increasingly run their own organizational branding on social media, using generic platforms such as Facebook, Twitter or Instagram and professional networks, such as LinkedIn. Moreover, through the use of artificial intelligence algorithms, organizations may use available data concerning the resumé, job profiles or LinkedIn activity in order to find suitable candidates (Trost, 2020).

After identifying suitable candidates, companies typically organize interviews, both HR and job-related, with short-listed candidates. This offers the opportunity to build a positive candidate experience early on in the process, which can shape not only immediate recruitment but also long-term talent commitment and retention. From the candidate's point of view, the three most important criteria concerning recruitment include speed, transparency and appreciation (Trost, 2020). Speed is defined by the organization's reaction to candidates' actions or decisions during the recruitment process whereas a transparent process means that candidates are always up to date with respect to the current status of their application and selection process. Appreciation involves treating each candidate with respect and consideration.

Given the role of recruiters in introducing the organization to external stakeholders and candidates, combined with the opportunity to establish a positive psychological contract (Rousseau et al., 2018), it is important for recruiters to be given appropriate tools to implement good talent attraction practices (Jepsen & Grob, 2015). As tools, companies may use attractive interviewing rooms with generous displays in order to facilitate project presentation and a detailed job description, or interactive playrooms for a comfortable discussion. During COVID-19, specific online tools to organize and carry out the interviews, such as virtual candidate experience rooms, have been created. New research regarding the use of innovative strategies to interview talent is discussed in a recent study conducted by Etzold et al. (2020), which shows that video interviews could reveal candidates' emotions such as happiness, surprise or fear. Nevertheless, there are critical agility competencies that are important for digital talent's recruitment during stress and uncertainty, such as tolerance for ambiguity, resilience and curiosity. These abilities are particularly relevant for talent working in multicultural settings (Caligiuri et al., 2020). Moreover, the selection process is a question of organizational and cultural fit that includes, but goes beyond technical expertise. External digital talent does not only need to possess the required technical and interpersonal skills, but they also need to be compatible with the firm's organizational culture. Therefore, companies may not necessarily choose the best qualified candidate in terms of abilities and skills, but the one who best suits their organizational and job-related requirements. Agile organizations are the first who strive to identify candidates that fit the company as a whole. They do this by not leaving the selection decision solely to the hiring manager, but also involving other personnel and departments in the decision-making process (Trost, 2020).

However, all such practices may not be enough if the profile searched for is particularly difficult to identify and attract. Therefore, companies operating in globally competitive industries could build a larger talent pool from their own database. They may also develop partnerships with start-ups and freelancers willing to get involved in critical projects for a certain period of time. This trend has been particularly salient as part of the emerging 'gig economy', which challenges existing business models and offers both opportunities and threats to organizations, industries and talent alike (Healy et al., 2017; Prassl, 2018). Companies may also develop a close collaboration with formerly employed digital talent who presently either has their own business or made the decision to work as freelancers. This strategy can become a good opportunity to develop alternative talent attraction strategies to support critical projects or short-term project tasks, when external recruitment is not suitable due to costs and time. This approach has become increasingly popular during COVID-19. Spurk and Straub (2020) found that most media accounts highlighted the effects of COVID-19 on changes in work arrangements for professionals and managers with a regular employment relationship, but paid significantly less attention to other forms of work. This same study showed that companies also use strategies for experts who have flexible employment relationships, such as temporary agency work and other forms of subcontracted labor, as well as work carried out under gig economy arrangements (Prassl, 2018). Some digital talent may therefore include a distinctive group of gig economy professionals, known as crowdsourced employees, who are recruited to perform freelance tasks (Ford et al., 2015; Schroeder et al., 2021).

By putting together the above findings from the literature that reflect talent recruitment and selection strategies in IT&C companies, we outline the following practices that could be integrated in the digital talent management process to improve digital talent attraction:

- Building partnerships with technical institutes and universities and organizing internship programs;
- Creating a compelling digital talent value proposition coupled with a strong employer brand by offering a realistic and genuine promise that could be attractive in the eyes of candidates;
- Adopting talent management practices that are valuable to prospective digital talent, such as compensation level, professional development and career path, attractiveness of the task and project, team professionalism and working with high-class specialists;
- Using specific recruitment tools, such as existing candidate database combined with specific additional approaches, such as recruiting formerly employed digital talent and freelancers, and collaborating with start-ups that operate within the same ecosystem;
- Using social media platforms, such as Facebook, Twitter and Instagram and career networks, such as LinkedIn, to communicate the organizational brand and identify suitable talent;
- Using artificial intelligence and algorithmic techniques to find suitable candidates;
- Building a positive candidate experience by integrating speed, transparency and appreciation in the recruitment and selection process;
- Creating a positive psychological contract by providing recruiters with adequate digital talent attraction resources and tools;
- Focusing on generic management and interpersonal competencies, in addition to technical expertise, including tolerance for ambiguity, resilience and curiosity.

Digital talent attraction also involves an induction and onboarding process, which raises the question of how to bring recruited digital talent to an appropriate level of productivity and job satisfaction in a timely and effective manner. Organizations focus their attention not only on developing recruitment practices, but also on attracting talent through the onboarding phase, which could determine whether digital talent is convinced enough to stay over the medium and long term (Joseph & Sandhya Sridevi, 2015). Onboarding refers to a structured framework of new hire assimilation focused on engaging with and integrating newcomers within the organization. It involves preparing them to succeed in their job in order to become productive members of the organization. An onboarding program needs to aim at building loyalty, accelerating performance early on, and eventually improving overall productivity and retention over the medium and long term (Joseph & Sandhya Sridevi, 2015). In relation to the 'hard' and 'soft' dimensions of onboarding, there are two possible reactions of a company regarding a mistake on the part of newcomers: either the company teaches them the basic, technical, methodical and professional skills and the rest comes from the actual practical experience or the company sees onboarding primarily as a social process by conveying aspects of interpersonal relationships. The latter direction is used by agile companies (Trost, 2020). Considering that competent human resources are one of the key drivers of competitive advantage across different industries, effective induction and onboarding of digital talent are critically important. Choosing between formal and informal onboarding; modeling the process for digital talent who works in ongoing digital product development processes; and performing onboarding in distributed environments, both locally and remotely (Britto et al., 2018) are important aspects that need to be taken into consideration when analyzing and performing digital talent onboarding. Britto et al. (2018) analyzed onboarding practices for software developers who work in globally distributed projects, highlighting the following induction practices that have a bearing on digital talent management: explaining job expectations to new hires; acknowledging the importance of formalizing and mirroring the onboarding program across sites; providing transparency within the project organization; clarifying key roles across sites; investing in traveling; providing extensive coaching and support in legacy projects; tailoring the training program according to software developers' needs; and using effective ways to provide meaningful feedback.

In the COVID-19 context, some of the abovementioned practices should be redefined and reinvented, given that workplace arrangements changed as the pandemic broke out (Chowell & Mizumoto, 2020). Remote onboarding presents unique challenges in comparison to local onboarding. Findings from 267 new hires at Microsoft presented in

Rodeghero et al. (2020) showed that the best digital talent attraction practices for software developers during this extraordinary context referred to promoting communication and asking for help when needed; encouraging teams to turn cameras on; scheduling one-to-one meetings; providing information about the organization; assigning onboarding buddies and technical mentors; emphasizing team building; supporting multiple onboarding tracks; and starting with simple tasks and providing updated documentation along the way. This research study recommended that for onboarding to be effective it needs to follow a clear process that is easily modifiable based on the new hires' needs. Other companies, for example, Twitter and Square, found that remote work was sufficient and announced that their staff could continue to work from home indefinitely (Brownlee, 2020). Another challenge regarding the onboarding process refers to the onboarding of senior digital talent, junior digital talent and digital talent with management responsibilities. In a non-crisis environment, a 'real touch' with the organizational context, people and specific projects, uniquely enabled by physical presence, could contribute to successful induction. Remote work may have impacted the effectiveness of talent induction programs and companies need to redefine their approach to onboarding.

To summarize, during a period of global stress and uncertainty, organizations could apply the following induction and onboarding practices in order to improve digital talent attraction:

- Identifying and clarifying expectations from both the organization and digital talent, during the recruitment process so that they can be mirrored in the onboarding phase;
- Promoting communication and one-to-one online meetings in an efficient and effective way;
- Assigning onboarding buddies and technical mentors;
- Providing updated documentation;
- Organizing a knowledge transfer plan for each newcomer;
- Organizing different onboarding plans for junior and senior digital talent, as well as for digital talent with management responsibilities.

Digital Talent Development

The process of digital talent management depends on implementing effective digital talent development that consists of strategies and practices, such as professional development, career advancement, compensation, benefits and use of tailored rewards that aim to nurture digital talent and enhance their organizational and job-related satisfaction. This section begins with a literature overview of specific digital talent development strategies and continues with the impact of motivation on digital talent management. In current organizational practice, learning is only partly associated with formal education and no longer perceived as a pre-career path, as there has been a noticeable shift from job security to the requirement for lifelong learning (Nilsson & Ellstrom, 2012). Considering the dynamic nature of knowledge-intensive industries and the rapid pace of technological development, organizations operating across such industries are faced with the need to provide and facilitate development opportunities for their digital talent. This is particularly crucial in view of digital talent's interest in and propensity toward learning and professional development (Barrett, 2004; Dekas et al., 2013). Thus, it is important for organizations to provide such opportunities in order to nurture and retain their digital talent (Cho & McLean, 2009). Talent development involves both formal and informal programs, such as short-term assignments, coaching, mentoring and training programs (Caligiuri et al., 2009). These programs may target the development of both technical and general management skills, which have become increasingly important to digital work (Marks & Scholarios, 2008). In particular, developing high-quality digital products and services has been a high priority to the IT&C industry, and solid technical expertise has been key in this regard. However, there has been growing research on the nature of digital work and productivity patterns pointing to the importance of a variety of 'soft' skills. Such skills are related to interpersonal communication, teamwork, project management and problem solving, and include the ability to adapt to different work arrangements and be open and flexible toward organizational change (Ahmed, 2013). In terms of technical skills, Florea and Stray (2019) analyzed 400 job adverts in 33 countries and mapped a skill taxonomy for software testers. Their findings suggest that companies operating in this specific area of digital work are mostly interested in test planning and design; test automation; functional testing; performance testing; and progress reporting.

The importance of digital talent development stems from the observation that developing digital abilities, competencies and skills involves not only attracting new digital talent, but also internally developing the required talent (Ready & Peebles, 2015). Digital talent development may include the need for reskilling programs and a redesign of work processes for reducing the gap between job requirements and existing knowledge and expertise (Karacay, 2017). There are risks, however, regarding such programs considering the dynamism of technological development (Bidwell, 2011). Some companies see digitalization as an opportunity to enhance talent's skillset and gain a competitive edge while others rely more on formal education, which increasingly is called to offer tailored programs that respond to shifting market needs (Hubschmid-Vierheilig et al., 2020). Studies examining the impact of development practices on talent's commitment and retention within IT&C companies found that career planning and development; performance appraisal and development; the use of reward and recognition; and training and learning are the most relevant practices that increase performance in the IT&C industry (Uraon, 2018; Uraon & Gupta, 2019). Companies are themselves learning organizations. A recent research among human resource development professionals in German-speaking countries found that when it comes to digital transformation, such professionals need to understand the functionality of smart machines and augmentation strategies to develop strategies focused on fusion skills and augmentation practices, and in this way to contribute to organizational learning and development (Meier et al., 2021). Moreover, artificial intelligence skills and agile ways of working are becoming increasingly important to organizations (Boston Consulting Group, 2019). Given that telework arrangements have become more important as a result of COVID-19, many organizations have switched to on-demand and self-paced trainings to cope with the new situation. Virtual training platforms offer both organizations and staff the opportunity to learn, interact and share demos. Such learning platforms and opportunities are not new to digital talent, who has traditionally used online forums and informal, peer-to-peer learning to acquire new knowledge, develop new expertise and keep abreast of the latest technologies. The proliferation of open-source software is a case in point. Digital talent contributes, often free of charge, both as individual users and in online communities, to technological development and in so doing both their own learning and that of their peers grow (von Hippel, 2016).

To sum up, facing the challenge of managing digital talent, who thrives in learning and exhibits a high propensity toward professional and career development, organizations can contribute to digital talent development by providing:

- Learning and training opportunities that are inspiring and relevant to digital talent's professional and career development;
- Career planning that includes the development of both technical and general management skills;
- Opportunities to develop new skillsets that reflect the latest trends, including artificial intelligence and agile ways of working;
- Performance appraisal that is centered on learning and development;
- Rewards and recognition schemes that are tailored to digital talent's needs and career goals;
- Learning platforms where digital talent can learn from peers and contribute to peer-to-peer learning;
- Partnerships with educational institutions.

Furthermore, motivation is intrinsically related to digital talent attraction, development and retention. Increased motivation can have a direct impact on digital talent's productivity and organizational and job satisfaction (Verner et al., 2014). Digital talent has different motivation triggers compared to professionals and managers who perform other roles and tasks. In an extensive systematic literature review, Beecham et al. (2008) found that software engineers are likely to be motivated by three interrelated factors: their special 'characteristics', such as their need for variety; their internal 'controls' that reflect their distinctive personality; and external 'moderators' that refer, inter alia, to career stage. The study showed that there are certain job-related dimensions and tasks that motivate software engineers, such as problem solving, working to the benefit of others and overcoming technical challenges. These findings are reflected to a good extent in other research, which found that software engineers are motivated by a variety of organizational, job-related and individual factors (Sharp et al., 2009). These include a close identification with the task; existence of a technical challenge; good management that is based on mutual trust and respect; existence of a career development path; variety of work; a sense of belonging and identification with the organization/team; rewards and recognition of performance; work-life balance; work autonomy, empowerment and responsibility; and the opportunity to make an impact.

Practices that organizations can put in place in order to create a motivating work environment and improve digital talent's motivation and satisfaction include creating clear growth perspectives within the organization; communicating organizational, team and individual goals, which is required given digital talent's strong technical and goal-centered orientation; the existence of external opportunities that provide development opportunities beyond those available within the company; and creating team cohesion, which is associated with a pleasant, sociable environment in which team members offer and receive mutual support and consideration (Cesar et al., 2014). Nevertheless, motivation alone cannot ensure adequate digital talent retention. Practices that aim to increase digital talent's motivation need to be supported by proactive managerial interventions that do not only aim to increase motivation, but also to qualitatively improve communication, opportunities for expressing, creativity and the nature and type of work. Such factors can have a positive impact on individual and team productivity and organizational commitment (Cesar et al., 2014). These practices also need to include respect for work-life balance, which is a factor that is highly important for digital talent, considering the dynamic, intense and demanding nature of their work (Boston Consulting Group, 2019). By appreciating digital talent's need for work-life balance, organizations communicate a powerful message, that is, that individual life plans include not only work, but also family, friends, religion or hobbies (Trost, 2020). Although companies used home-office models as a motivation and retention tool before COVID-19, the pandemic pushed companies to ensure the necessary conditions for remote work. This shift has brought about a new set of practices that aim to increase well-being and motivation in critical times (Ralph et al., 2020). Remote work, however, can also have important benefits that increase digital talent's motivation, such as time savings due to less commuting; a higher degree of flexibility and work autonomy; and financial savings (Russo et al., 2020). Granting a higher degree of work autonomy and flexibility, in particular, can have a positive impact on motivation and well-being.

In conclusion, motivation is an essential component of digital talent development and has a direct impact on job satisfaction and organizational commitment and retention. Organizations can motivate digital talent by employing strategies and practices that involve:

- Good management that is based on mutual trust and respect;
- A clear and rewarding career development path;
- Interesting projects, tasks and work variety;
- Rewards and recognition schemes;
- Work-life balance;
- Empowerment, responsibility and work autonomy;
- Protecting and improving well-being during critical and turbulent times.

References

Ahmed, F. (2013). Soft Skills and Software Development: A Reflection from the Software Industry. *Electrical and Computer Engineering Publications, 40*. https://ir.lib.uwo.ca/electricalpub/40

Alias, N. E., Nor, N. M., & Hassan, R. (2016). *Chapter 9 The Relationships Between Talent Management Practices, Employee Engagement, and Employee Retention in the Information and Technology (IT) Organizations in Selangor*. Springer.

Barinova, E. P., Sheremetyeva, E. N., & Zotova, A. S. (2020). *Digital Talents: Realities and Prospects in Digital Age: Chances, Challenges and Future*. Springer. https://doi.org/10.1007/978-3-030-27015-5

Barrett, R. (2004). Working at Webboyz: An Analysis of Control Over the Software Development Labour. *Sociology, 38*(4), 777–794.

Beecham, S., Baddoo, N., Hall, T., Robinson, H., & Sharp, H. (2008). Motivation in Software Engineering: A Systematic Literature Review. *Information and Software Technology, 50*(9–10), 860–878. https://doi.org/10.1016/j.infsof.2007.09.004

Bidwell, M. J. (2011). Paying more to get less: The Effects of External Hiring versus Internal Mobility. *Administrative Science Quarterly, 56*(3), 369–407.

Boston Consulting Group. (2019). *Decoding Digital Talent, What 27,000 Digital Experts in 180 Countries Tell Us About Their Mobility and Work Preferences*. Boston Consulting Group & the Network.

Britto, R., Cruzes, D. S., Smite, D., & Sablis, A. (2018). Onboarding Software Developers and Teams in Three Globally Distributed Legacy Projects: A Multi-Case Study. *Journal of Software: Evolution and Process, 30*, e1921. https://doi.org/10.1002/smr.1921

Brownlee, D. (2020, May). Twitter, Square Announce Work From Home Forever Option: What Are The Risks? [Online]. https://www.forbes.com/sites/danabrownlee/2020/05/18/twitter-square-announce-work-from-home-forever-optionwhat-are-the-risks/?sh=64c876762565

Caligiuri, P., De Cieri, H., Minbaeva, D., Verbeke, A., & Zimmermann, A. (2020). International HRM Insights for Navigating the COVID-19 Pandemic: Implications for Future Research and Practice. *Journal of International Business Studies, 51*, 697–713. https://doi.org/10.1057/s41267-020-00335-9

Caligiuri, P., Tarique, I., & Jacobs, R. (2009). Selection for International Assignments. *Human Resource Management Review, 19*(3), 251–262.

Cesar, A., da Silva, F. Q. B., Felix, A. d. L. C., & Carneiro, D. E. S. (2014). Motivation in Software Engineering Industrial Practice: A Cross-Case Analysis of Two Software Organisations. *Information and Software Technology, 56*, 79–101. https://doi.org/10.1016/j.infsof.2013.06.006

Cho, Y., & McLean, G. N. (2009). Leading Asian countries' HRD practices in the IT industry: A comparative study of South Korea and India. *Human Resource Development International, 12*, 313–331. https://doi.org/10.1080/13678860902982108

Chowell, G., & Mizumoto, K. (2020). The COVID-19 Pandemic in the USA: What Might We Expect? *The Lancet, 395*(10230), 1093–1094.

Claus, L. (2019). HR Disruption—Time Already to Reinvent Talent Management. *BRQ Business Research Quarterly, 22*, 207–215. https://doi.org/10.1016/j.brq.2019.04.002

Corporate Leadership Council. (2004). *Driving Performance and Retention Through Employee Engagement*. Corporate Executive Board.

Dekas, K. H., Bauer, T. N., & Welle, B. (2013). Organizational Citizenship Behavior, Version 2.0: A Review and Qualitative Investigation of OCBs for Knowledge Workers at Google and Beyond. *Academy of Management Perspectives, 27*(3), 219–237.

Etzold, V., Wanner, T., & Butz, L. (2020). WAR FOR TALENTS MEETS FACIAL EXPRESSION—Leveraging Recruiting Videos in Professional Service Firms. *Procedia Computer Science, 176*, 1783–1792.

Flecker, J. (Ed.). (2018). *Space, Place and Global Digital Work, Dynamics of Virtual Work*. Palgrave Macmillan. https://doi.org/10.1057/978-1-137-48087-3_5

Florea, R., & Stray, V. (2019). The Skills That Employers Look for in Software Testers. *Software Quality Journal, 27*, 1449–1479. https://doi.org/10.1007/s11219-019-09462-5

Ford, R. C., Richard, B., & Ciuchta, M. P. (2015). Crowdsourcing: A New Way of Employing Non-Employees? *Business Horizons, 58*, 377–388.

Gilch, P. M., & Sieweke, J. (2020). Recruiting Digital Talent: The Strategic Role of Recruitment in Organisations' Digital Transformation. *German Journal of Human Resource Management*. https://doi.org/10.1177/2397002220952734

Halme, K., & Niinikoski, M.-L. (2019). *Innovation Policy to Renew the Economy and Society. Publications of the Ministry of Economic Affairs and Employment, 2019:7*. Government of Finland.

Healy, J., Nicholson, D., & Pekarek, A. (2017). Should We Take the Gig Economy Seriously? *Labour & Industry: A Journal of the Social and Economic Relations of Work, 27*(3), 232–248.

Hubschmid-Vierheilig, E., Rohrer, M., & Mitsakis, F. (2020). *Digital Competence Revolution and Human Resource Development in the United Kingdom and Switzerland* (Vol. I). Springer International Publishing, in The Future of HRD. https://doi.org/10.1007/978-3-030-52410-4_3

Jepsen, D. M., & Grob, S. (2015). Sustainability in Recruitment and Selection: Building a Framework of Practices. *SAGE Publications, 9*(2), 160–178. https://doi.org/10.1177/0973408215588250

Joseph, D., & Sandhya Sridevi, M. (2015). Effective Onboarding as a Talent Management Tool for Employee Retention. *International Journal in Management and Social Science, 03*(07), 175–186.

Karacay, G. (2017). *Talent Development for Industry 4.0*. Springer. https://doi.org/10.1007/978-3-319-57870-5_7

Marks, A., & Scholarios, D. (2008). Choreographing A System: Skill and Employability in Software Work. *Economic and Industrial Democracy, 29*(1), 96–124.

Meier, C., Seufert, S., Guggemos, J., & Spirgi, J. (2021). Learning Organizations in the Age of Smart Machines. In D. Ifenthaler, S. Hofhues, M. Egloffstein, & C. Helbig (Eds.), *Digital Transformation of Learning Organizations*. Springer. https://doi.org/10.1007/978-3-030-55878-9_5.

Montandon, J.-E., Politowski, C., Silva, L. L., & Valente, M. T. (2021). What Skills do IT Companies Look for in New Developers? A Study with Stack Overflow Jobs. *Information and Software Technology, 129*, 106429. https://doi.org/10.1016/j.infsof.2020.106429

Niculescu, A., Negoita, O. D., Popescu, M. A.-M., & Purcărea, A. A. (2019). The Impact of Psychological Factors on Employees in the IT&C Environment. *Studies in Informatics and Control, 28*(1), 77–86.

Nilsson, S., & Ellstrom, P. E. (2012). Employability and Talent Management: Challenges for HRD Practices. *European Journal of Training and Development, 36*(1), 26–45.

Prassl, J. (2018). *Humans as a Service: The Promise and Perils of Work in the Gig Economy*. Oxford University Press.

Ralph, P., Baltes, S., Adisaputri, G., Torkar, R., Kovalenko, V., Kalinowski, M., Novielli, N., Yoo, S., Devroey, X., Tan, X., Zhou, M., Turhan, B., Hoda, R., Hata, H., Robles, G., Fard, A. M., & Alkadhi, R. (2020). Pandemic Programming How COVID-19 Affects Software Developers and How Their Organizations Can Help. *Empirical Software Engineering, 25*, 4927–4961. https://doi.org/10.1007/s10664-020-09875-y

Ready, D. A., & Peebles, M. E. (2015). Developing the next generation of enterprise leaders. *MIT Sloan Management Review, 57*(1), 43–51.

Rodeghero, P., Zimmermann, T., Houck, B., & Ford, D (2020). *Please Turn Your Cameras On: Remote Onboarding of Software Developers During a Pandemic.* Retrieved January 22, 2021, from https://arxiv.org/pdf/2011.08130v1.pdf

Rodrigues, J. A., & Naidoo, E. (2016). Performance and Talent: Essentials of Talent Development Programs and Groups. In M. Zeuch (Ed.), *Handbook of Human Resources Management.* Springer. https://doi.org/10.1007/978-3-662-44152-7_40

Rousseau, D., Hansen, S., & Tomprou, M. (2018). A Dynamic Phase Model of Psychological Contract Processes. *Journal of Organizational Behaviour, 39*(9), 1081–1098.

Russo, D., Hanel, P. H. P., Altnickel, S., & van Berkel, N. (2020). Predictors of Well-being and Productivity of Software Professionals During the COVID-19 Pandemic—A Longitudinal Study. Retrieved January 1, 2020, from https://arxiv.org/pdf/2007.12580.pdf

Schroeder, A. N., Bricka, T. M., & Whitaker, J. H. (2021). Work Design in a Digitized Gig Economy. *Human Resource Management Review, 31*(1), 100692. https://doi.org/10.1016/j.hrmr.2019.100692

Sharp, H., Baddoo, N., Beecham, S., Hall, T., & Robinson, H. (2009). Models of Motivation in Software Engineering. *Information and Software Technology, 51,* 219–233. https://doi.org/10.1016/j.infsof.2008.05.009

Sparrow, P., & Makram, H. (2015). What Is the Value of Talent Management? Building Value-Driven Processes Within a Talent Management Architecture. *Human Resource Management Review, 25*(3), 249–263.

Spurk, D., & Straub, C. (2020). Flexible Employment Relationships and Careers in Times of the COVID-19 Pandemic. *Journal of Vocational Behavior, 119,* 103435. https://doi.org/10.1016/j.jvb.2020.103435

Tikhonov, A. (2019). Applying of Employer Branding System in the IT-Companies' Human Resource Management. *ESPACIOS Magazine, 40*(38), 23.

Trost, A. (2020). *Human Resources Strategies Balancing Stability and Agility in Times of Digitization.* Springer. https://doi.org/10.1007/978-3-030-30592-5.

Uraon, R. S. (2018). Examining the Impact of HRD Practices on Organizational Commitment and Intention to Stay Within Selected Software Companies in India. *Advances in Developing Human Resources, 20*(1), 11–43. https://doi.org/10.1177/1523422317741691

Uraon, R. S., & Gupta, M. (2019). Do HRD Practices Affect Perceived Market Performance Through Operational Performance? Evidence from Software Industry. *International Journal of Productivity and Performance Management, 69*(1), 85–108. https://doi.org/10.1108/IJPPM-06-2018-0207

Verner, J. M., Babarc, M. A., Cerpad, N., Halle, T., & Beechamf, S. (2014). Factors that Motivate Software Engineering Teams: A Four Country Empirical Study. *Journal of Systems and Software, 92*, 115–127. https://doi.org/10.1016/j.jss.2014.01.008

von Hippel, E. (2016). *Free Innovation*. MIT Press.

Xu, H., Wu, D., Xing, L., & Huang, L. (2017). The Talent Planning Model and Empirical Research to the Key Disciplines in Science and Technology. *Cluster Computing, 20*, 3275–3286. https://doi.org/10.1007/s10586-017-1060-8

CHAPTER 4

Attracting, Developing and Retaining Digital Talent: Empirical Evidence

Abstract While talent management emerged and later developed as a focus in both the academics' and practitioners' agendas, companies continue to face challenges in implementing talent management strategies. This is particularly the case with respect to digital talent and the use of digital talent management that takes into account and decidedly integrates the distinctive nature of digital talent into talent management strategies and practices in a human-centered way. Aiming to balance the early normative approaches in talent management, this chapter integrates the scholarly perspective with empirical evidence on the effective digital talent management practices implemented by information and communication technology (IT&C) companies. Balancing the organizational and individual perspective, the chapter provides insights on effective practices to attract, develop and retain digital talent, based on a qualitative research design that included individual interviews with representatives of the management of IT&C companies, HR staff and IT&C professionals.

Keywords Digital talent management (DTM) • Digital talent attraction • Digital talent development • Digital talent retention • Empirical evidence

Despite the rich literature on managing talent, organizations continue to face critical challenges in implementing talent management strategies

S. Dan et al., *Digital Talent Management*,
https://doi.org/10.1007/978-3-030-76750-1_4

(Björkman et al., 2017). A PWC report addressing challenges identified at global level stressed out the lack of available competencies and skills as a major limit for the growth of their businesses (PWC, 2017). Moreover, in knowledge-intensive industries, such as the information and communication technology (IT&C) industry, besides talent shortages, managing digital talent is identified as a key challenge (Chaudhuri et al., 2018). While talent management practices are generally built around corporate agendas (Minbaeva & Vardi, 2019), studies advocate for the need to balance the organizational and individual perspectives to achieve successful implementation (Farndale et al., 2014). To address this call, in this chapter, we provide empirical evidence on the key areas of talent management applied to digital talent from the perspective of both individual digital talent and organizations.

Considering the particularities of digital talent outlined earlier in Chap. 2 (as abstract thinkers, up to date with the latest technologies, but on the other hand as individuals who know and assert their value and have high expectations from their employer) and the changes posed by COVID-19, companies are required to build an effective, well-adjusted strategy to attract, develop and retain them. The pandemic context brought about even greater challenges to attract, develop and retain digital talent. Based on individual interviews with IT&C professionals and managers, HR staff, and executives of IT&C companies, this chapter highlights key empirical findings on the practices used by the IT&C companies included in our sample for attracting, developing and retaining digital talent.

Digital Talent Retention

The retention of digital talent is particularly critical considering global talent shortages and the tough market competition. Globally competitive markets lead to the majority of IT&C companies providing various benefits to digital talent, stressing the need to differentiate themselves in order to effectively manage digital talent. Traditionally, in non-COVID-19 times, from an HR perspective, the differentiation strategy used to be based on creating a good work environment, which not only comprised the physical space (comfortable and good aesthetics of the office spaces, easy access location close to the city center), but also good work conditions: "*They stay because they feel we are close to them, they feel they are listened to and heard here, that there is always someone they can get to when facing a problem, because they have a good relationship with the team, they need to be seen and understood, and this is happening here*" (HR Manager, 2 years in the company, F, SAP). The switch, almost entirely, to remote work required the identification of new strategies for creating a good work environment. Working from home means fewer possibilities for a company to influence work conditions. Digital talent needed to adjust their home conditions to their work, by reorganizing the space to fit a home office. This involved not only the physical space but also a space to prevent interruptions and various possible disruptions. Companies focused mainly on providing the necessary technical equipment (computer device, accessories, access to online platforms) and paid less attention to supporting digital talent in managing the space and the other facilities that are required for home-office work.

The impact of digital talent retention strategies seems to vary as a function of digital talent's level of seniority and experience in a given company. The COVID-19 context made newly hired digital talent more focused on keeping their jobs and obtaining a secure job. Due to the common practice of laying off the latest hired digital talent in case of restructuring, the talent who was hired more recently was more focused on their job security. More experienced digital talent shows higher expectations for learning and development, which confers them a sense of progress. In non-COVID-19 times, an effective strategy that contributes to digital talent retention resides in flexible work arrangements (the possibility to opt for a type of contract which allows work from home) and high individual autonomy. The pandemic accentuated the need for flexibility and made the flexible arrangement even more flexible: "*The anniversary feedback meetings and the exit interviews show that our talent appreciates the fact they can work from home, that they have this flexibility and more freedom. They are required to get to the office only when the customer gets here or when they have scheduled meetings. The pandemic made flexible arrangements even more flexible*" (Workforce Manager, 2 years in the company, F, user interface (UI)/user experience (UX)); "*There is a young atmosphere and a flexible work schedule. I use this option and I like it. I would enjoy even more days working from home. I am more productive when working from home; it saves the time for traveling to work. There are persons who are not that productive, but I work pretty well from home*" (Consultant, 5 years in the company, F, SAP). A benefit of the approach focused on flexibility is related to an implicit assumption of digital talent's assumed responsibility. Shifting the accountability for achieving the planned objectives toward digital talent empowers them and has further positive implications on engagement and job satisfaction: "*Talent has flexible arrival time. But when they have a scheduled meeting, they will be there. It is an issue assumed by both parties. Flexibility comes with a certain level of accountability expectations*" (Workforce Manager, UI/UX, 6 years in the company). During COVID-19, most of the IT&C companies implement remote work arrangements and try to ensure more flexibility. This is achieved not only through decision-making power over one's own tasks, but also through freedom of self-expression and openness to diversity: "*This company is a place that always inspired us. There is no dress code, so one can dress as one wishes, even when one goes to the office. I listen to metal music and I wear a death head t-shirt, but I am appreciated here for the skills I have*" (Consultant, 2 years, Senior, 2 years, M, SAP).

While flexible work arrangements are acknowledged as an efficient strategy to motivate digital talent, they also have associated downsides, such as the perceived lack of control over digital talent's work; the need to adjust to a new management style; the need to adjust the schedules for team-based activities; facing potential customer complaints; resentment amongst the staff for whom flexibility is not possible; diminishing of team cohesiveness; and reduced communication and knowledge exchange, which might negatively impact project coordination. From the digital talent's point of view, teamwork with the registered sole traders, who work as freelancers, implies certain communication difficulties and insufficient information about their availability: "*Some PFA take advantage and we do not know if they get in or not, even if it is easier face to face. Sometimes it is not clear if they are available or not*" (Team Leader, Senior, 2 years in the company, M, UI/UX). To counteract the potential risks, before COVID-19, companies implemented several strategies, such as using more time at the office in the early stage after starting employment to facilitate the integration of new colleagues into the team, organizing events for both the digital talent who works remotely and talent who works in the office. These practices aimed to support a good interaction and work relationships from the very beginning and to help establishing a good connection with the other team members. The pandemic brought about even greater challenges in managing work from home: "*Since the pandemic, the company aims to support its talent by allowing them to adapt their schedule to their own home responsibilities, such as synchronizing their work schedule with the children's kindergarten schedule*" (HR Professional, 3 years in the company, F).

This practice is strongly linked to another important factor that positively influences retention—the cohesiveness of the team, which is an important motivating factor to remain in the company for both junior and senior digital talent: "*I constantly see them spending time together, they are well bound. One of the team members who wanted to leave the company changed her mind in the last day*" (Workforce Manager, 3 years in the company, F, UI/UX); "*For me, the team I work with is important. I had bigger opportunities to work in other companies, on higher level positions, but I enjoy working with the team here. I like the manager I work with*" (Team Leader, 2 years in the company, Senior, F, SAP). When the company uses work in office, the strategy recommended to the company consists of creating opportunities for digital talent to better know each other, to interact and communicate more by means of mentoring sessions and trainings delivered by the seniors: "*We are over 900 people, and it is difficult for everyone to know each other, but training colleagues could insist on trainings in which seniors could teach juniors and collaborate with the university, which might help on the long term*" (Workforce Manager, UI/UX). When digital talent works mainly remotely, the challenges to achieve team cohesiveness are even higher. The role of the leadership and direct supervisors becomes even more important to ensure good communication and interaction: "*Caring for digital talent, and not merely teambuilding activities, is extremely important during the pandemic*" (HR Professional, 4 years' experience in the company, F).

As a means to retain digital talent, the company offers numerous benefits: "*We have more benefits here than in other companies, such as private insurance, sports facilities, vouchers to events, sports rooms, 7card*" (Team Leader, Senior, 5 years in the company, M, SAP). While this is attractive, given the fact that there are so many types of benefits, it is difficult for digital talent to be aware of them all or to benefit from all of them: "*We have so many benefits. The truth is, we have some colleagues who are not interested, who never benefited from 10% discounts on anything*" (Workforce Manager, UI/UX). On the other hand, management is aware that all IT&C companies provide various benefits to their digital talent, and as a result this is not a differentiating strategy anymore. For this reason, companies try to identify strategies that are more effective at boosting digital talent's motivation. Performance appraisal is generally associated with rewards. Given the importance of this process for digital talent, there are high expectations for a fair and rewarding performance evaluation process. In the cases when the team leader does not have sufficient time to schedule individual meetings with each digital talent, there is a high risk of individual and/or collective complaints and dissatisfaction: "*Interviews did not work that well because we did not have evaluation meetings and all colleagues complained, we had no time because we had project tasks to accomplish. Besides, there were colleagues who got here later this year and did not enter the evaluation process*" (Team Leader, Senior, 2 years in the company, M, UI/UX).

Job performance evaluation should also be differentiated as a function of the job level. For senior digital talent, the frequency of the evaluation meetings can be lower, that is, one evaluation meeting per year, while for junior talent, more meetings are recommended: "*Juniors need two performance appraisal meetings every year, because they need to know the level that they reached*" (Workforce Manager, UI/UX). Nonetheless, irrespective of the level of experience, digital talent expresses a strong need for getting more often in contact with their direct supervisors, which means that online one-to-one meetings are recommended. This requires more time allocated by team leaders for these individual meetings to express care and attention for their team members. Moreover, empirical evidence shows that during COVID-19, regardless of their experience level, digital talent expresses a general feeling of lack of communication with their direct supervisors. While the top management of the organization succeeds in maintaining communication at the organizational level and is focused on sharing information about the general progress of the company, digital talent feels a disconnection with their supervisor. To boost motivation and enhance retention, team leaders need to focus more attention on the members of their teams and improve the communication with them.

Digital Talent Attraction

Talent management practices target the recruitment of high potentials by building a strong employer image for sourcing talent at national and international levels (Sparrow & Makram, 2015). Aiming at a 'premium employer brand', companies in our sample implement various strategies to keep and increase their competitive advantage on the market: modern work conditions; central location; a focus on digital talent's work-life balance through a balanced workload; avoidance of overtime; integration of families in company events; diversity of projects and opportunities for digital talent to change projects and gain variety in their work; support for professional development related to various technologies and the provision of personal growth opportunities. The COVID-19 context brought about new challenges and pushed companies toward identifying new solutions to attract digital talent. When remote work becomes a common practice for most IT&C companies, the focus on providing attractive work facilities (such as central location, ergonomic offices, access to meal facilities, parking, etc.) needs to be replaced by different attraction strategies.

Despite a general increase in unemployment during COVID-19, dynamic and innovative industries, such as the IT&C industry, are still facing a high competition for digital talent: "*The competition for the best talent is as fierce as usual. While several small companies disappeared, the applicants are more reluctant to change their jobs during the pandemic. They do not want to take risks and if they do, they expect better payment*" (HR Professional, F, 4 years in the company). While, on the one hand, this could mean decreased staff fluctuation and lower turnover, on the other hand, it implies a more difficult and more costly recruitment process for filling in the vacancies. To succeed in attracting the required digital talent in a risky context requires companies to make even more attractive job offers. Furthermore, by taking the expression the 'war for talent' literally, a critical step is the sourcing and selection of digital talent. By using specific HR tools such as Success Factors, which allows the internal system to communicate with the company's career portal, combined with certain social media platforms, such as LinkedIn, the companies could better succeed in identifying the most suitable candidates. However, our empirical evidence suggests that the intense competition in digital talent recruitment transformed the recruitment process into a 'sales' process. Passive recruitment methods, such as online job posting became less effective and companies needed to implement more active recruitment methods. Recruiters, however, are required to have effective selling skills, to know very well the job profile, the particularities of the company and the content of projects that are likely to be assigned to the new recruit: "*A recruitment challenge in a competitive market resides in attracting candidates who fit the job requirements and convince them to have a first meeting with the recruiter. It does not necessarily result in getting the job immediately, but it allows candidates to know the company and the available opportunities*" (Workforce Manager, F, 3 years in the company). Persuasion skills are also considered to be relevant for recruiters to be able to transparently present the information about the job in such a manner as to convince suitable candidates. This helps candidates to form a correct mental picture of the job and address any misunderstandings that they might have about the job and future opportunities: "*There are candidates who enter the interview having a certain opinion: neutral, positive, or negative. And they tell you, this is what I heard … colleagues said this. But most of the times, they get to us and they realize that the negative opinions vary, and I keep telling them that it strongly depends on the type of project, manager, and colleagues, because there are 1700 of us here. My experience can be different compared to yours. I tell them: try to be objective. It is difficult to depict the right image from the beginning and besides, things change also*" (Workforce Manager, 5 years in the company, F, UI/UX).

However, despite the fact that IT&C companies face a tremendous competition when aiming to attract needed digital talent, an effective recruitment process should also contribute, from the early stages of the hiring process to the long-term retention of the new hires. This is facilitated when companies balance the attractiveness of the recruitment offer with a focus on offering accurate and transparent information about the organization and the job. To ensure a long-term relationship with the newly employed digital talent, recruiters need to correctly and realistically inform applicants about the job requirements and the company's strategic plans: "*We insist on transparency. If there are discrepancies between what the new hired person expects from the job content and the tasks that get assigned later, a strong dissatisfaction might appear and this often leads to early quitting. The recruiter should receive a clear job profile, in agreement with the hiring organization, in order to be able to clarify the job requirements with the applicant*" (Recruiter, 4 years in the company, F). Furthermore, the effectiveness of recruitment methods depends on the type of vacancy. For junior positions, classical recruitment methods such as posting job adverts on social media and collaborations with technical institutes and universities are still efficient. For successfully attracting senior digital talent, recruiters need to directly contact the candidates and use referrals to a larger extent than in the case of junior-level recruitment. The initial message, which includes relevant information about the job (technologies involved, tools, team particularities) and allows candidates to familiarize themselves with the job, needs to be followed by taking direct contact with the candidate in a timely manner.

Moreover, large-size companies need to manage the digital talent's role diversity that leads to large variations in recruitment needs. A significant resource that companies could benefit from resides in having an efficient recruitment team. In a growing company, recruitment is an important process for the business, and recruiters perceive themselves as being very useful for the company. Rival interests might exist between the HR staff and executives, the former being more oriented toward attracting high potential people, whereas the latter toward hiring within profitable financial business targets. While recruiters invest strong efforts in identifying and attracting valuable digital talent, the final decision makers might reject the applicants due to financial reasons: "*There is a connection between business and people; if you don't have people, one cannot do business, and if you don't do business, you cannot bring people in. It's a circular flow*" (Recruiter, 2 years in the company, F).

Both before and during COVID-19, resources that boost the attractiveness of the company are perceived differently as a function of the applicants' expertise. For young, entry-level newcomers, attractive resources are related to material and social resources. When the company uses less remote work, junior-level digital talent is attracted by good work conditions; aesthetics of the office space; access to entertainment rooms; social events; and competitions organized by the company. In addition, entry-level digital talent tends to be motivated by the possibility to use new technologies and perform challenging tasks. During critical times, when companies use remote work extensively, junior-level digital talent tends to be more interested in the payment level, job security, and the content of their work. Senior newcomers are strongly attracted by the available learning resources, which include the content of the project, learning opportunities and access to niche specialized resources in their field of interest: "*Senior-level digital talent is fascinated when you give them a challenging project, which allows them to grow from a technical point of view, so they feel they are learning; give them a Safari license, which allows them to learn, or provide them with access to technical conferences*" (Workforce Manager, 2 years in the company, F, UI/UX). Moreover, they are more interested in work-life balance and stability, and less in material resources, compared to juniors: "*The entry-level digital talent is attracted by the fact that there is one entire floor with relaxing areas and games, ping-pong, billiard facilities, and so forth ... for those who have time to go. I have been there less than twice in two years*" (Software Developer, Senior, 2 years in the company, M, SAP).

The employer brand represents an attraction strategy for both entry- and senior-level applicants: "*This company offers many opportunities and has many advantages: it is an important brand, acknowledged by its customers; it enjoys good publicity here in the city; and it has a good reputation among its digital talent. My friends would like to work here*" (Team Leader, Senior, 2 years in the company, M, UI/UX). IT&C companies build their internal employer brand by actively participating in regional and local urban life, through sponsorships, donations, sports and charitable events. By creating a good and friendly work atmosphere, with high digital talent autonomy, companies not only give their talent a sense of fulfillment, but they also build their 'employer brand', which further becomes a good attraction, and subsequently retention, strategy: "*When I came here, I had already known many digital talent who was already working here. They told me they were content with their employer and they felt well here, and the employer was taking care of them. They said that there are growing and development opportunities here and a higher salary than elsewhere*" (Software Developer, 2 years in the company, M, SAP). Being a large company and operating for a long time on the market, provide the advantage of being trustworthy and perceived as a secure workplace: "*It is a big company that inspires trust. For people it is important to get a secure job and projects that use new technologies so that one can learn new things*" (Team Leader, Senior, 5 years in the company, M, SAP).

Another strategy to attract digital talent is based on the possibility to change the project and/or job if not satisfied, which is an opportunity that particularly the digital talent who works in a large company has. Recruiters advertise this option as a special opportunity and the candidates develop expectations related to the chances of choosing other projects that better match their preferences. Furthermore, a good onboarding experience can contribute to managing digital talent over the medium and short term. Many of the IT&C companies in our sample are using a knowledge transfer plan in order to ensure a quick productivity of the newcomer by assigning a buddy, responsible for the social side of the integration, such as presenting the team members, and a technical mentor. Most analyzed companies also put together a plan for a step-by-step integration of newcomers into project work and specific tasks. One-to-one online meetings with team members, that are carried out not only as part of the agile way of working, but as an integral part of onboarding, seem to be effective at ensuring a successful onboarding experience.

Both in terms of onboarding and general work practices, there are differences between digital talent depending on their technical specialization and expertise, and these differences are correlated with specific individual and group characteristics: "*There are differences between the developers who write code all the time and the ones who work in SAP. The latter are specialized and do less technical work and are more open to communication*" (Recruiter, 2 years in the company, F, UI/UX). On the one hand, these differences have an impact on specific groups and types of digital talent and influence HR processes, such as the type of talent management approaches that are used and the way in which recruitment, induction, learning, development and retention practices are implemented. On the other hand, managing a growing company means standardizing processes and stabilizing activities in order to reduce discrepancies between existing procedures. However, the considerable group and individual differences that exist between digital talent imply that it is important for companies to develop and apply a customized approach to digital talent attraction that involves the use of tailored practices and interventions in a fair and equitable way.

Digital Talent Development

One debate in talent management practice refers to whether organizations should source talented professionals and managers externally or develop the required competencies and skills internally. Because of the increased costs of developing talent, an alternative solution is to buy the talent the company needs from the external market. However, the existing literature pinpoints the potential risks of unsuccessful integration of the sourced talent considering the particularities of the hiring company (Bidwell, 2011). In such a case the portability of the talent is questioned. The remaining option is to internally develop talent by focusing on identifying the need for talented staff and then investing in developing them (Ready & Peebles, 2015). Traditionally, talent development involves both informal and formal leadership programs, such as short-term assignments, coaching and mentoring, and training programs (Caligiuri et al., 2009).

The COVID-19 context triggered the need for a stronger organizational focus on talent development, which can be used as a strategy for motivating and retaining digital talent, as reviewed earlier in Chap. 3. Evidence from the individual interviews shows a stronger interest of experienced digital talent in development programs and obtaining additional qualifications. While during critical times organizations typically seek to reduce costs by cutting the budget allocated to trainings, our evidence shows that especially the experienced digital talent has tried to utilize the time saved by reduced commuting to and from work with participating in more online courses and workshops. In addition, many of the interviewed digital talent searched for online courses on their own and organized their own participation in these courses without necessarily relying on the company's financial support. Our empirical findings further show that there are situations when digital talent needs reskilling or a new certification and, in this context, development programs and strategies play an essential role that can strengthen their job satisfaction, organizational commitment and retention. Thus, career progression and growing opportunities represent an important digital talent management (DTM) strategy: "*In the company I was working at that moment, there was already a team leader and no one could replace him. That meant remaining a software developer because no one had any promotion opportunities as in a large company as this one*" (Team Leader, Senior, <2 years in the company, M, UI/UX); "*I like this company because I can grow here*" (Consultant, >5 years in the company, F, SAP).

As shown above, talent development represents an essential strategy that can 'make or break' digital talent management, considering the growing labor market requirements for digital talent and their propensity toward learning and career development. To seek to retain digital talent, the companies in our sample provide development opportunities and career paths, such as the 'technical guru' training program, which provides a path for advancing to management positions. The existence of opportunities to progress to leadership positions represents both a development and retention incentive since a higher position brings about new challenges and contributes to individual growth: "*I am not that interested in what is happening on the market now, mainly due to the moment I am in my career at this moment. I was offered a leadership position here. I used to be a technical lead, but now I am more focused on my professional and personal, and this is more challenging, and it helps me grow*" (Team Leader and Technical Leader, Senior, 2 years in the company, F, UI/UX). Development plans have a strong impact when they are built with a long-term perspective in mind, and for this reason training programs provided by companies need to be strategically planned and announced ahead of time: "*On the short term the information we get about trainings provided by the company are quite ok. We get an e-mail, we register to a training, and it is approved by someone. But on the long term … we do not really know what trainings will be available and it would be super to know this information in advance*" (Team Leader, Senior, 2 years in the company, M, UI/UX). In this way, digital talent can follow more precisely a long-term development and career path and plan in advance the trainings they need to reach their development goals. In terms of development opportunities, another attractive practice is related to the opportunity to develop international experience and to work on projects that involve collaboration with corporate headquarters. A side benefit of this practice is the opportunity to travel, which is highly valuable to digital talent, particularly those who have limited family responsibilities.

Given the high competition for digital talent worldwide, various alternative types of providers of specialized expertise appeared within the gig economy system. As an alternative form to regular employment, it has become more common for companies to search for required digital talent outside the organization, by subcontracting freelancers, start-ups and other types of short-term work arrangements. In this regard, a business growth mindset requires approaching these suppliers of expertise as valuable partners on the market and searching for ways to support their development. Companies could encourage the digital talent who no longer feels satisfied with their company and plans to leave, to initiate their own start-ups and continue collaboration in this way as part of the same business ecosystem. This represents a proactive form of retention of digital talent, which can become a win-win solution for both the company and individual digital talent. By taking a positive attitude to this type of turnover, companies can gain trustworthy partners, who are known to companies, and in this way they can continue to do business with them, instead of losing them, possibly to competing firms. Digital talent who finds themselves in such situations gain an increased degree of autonomy and a reliable client for their available expertise, which can ensure the sustainability of their new enterprise. However, for such alternative arrangements to retention to work effectively, mutual trust and consideration are required, along with a favorable attitude on both sides, which is not always the case in practice considering that turnover can be a result of dissatisfaction with the organization and its management as well as an outcome of interpersonal conflict. Thus, companies who are considering such collaborations need to perform an assessment of the likelihood of success of the collaboration and an analysis of possible benefits and risks.

To conclude, COVID-19 intensified particular motivation frames for digital talent, which have a bearing on talent management practices that aim to attract, develop and retain digital talent. Empirical data presented in this chapter evidenced a ***distinct novice digital talent motivation frame*** and a ***distinct entitled digital talent motivation frame***. Newly hired digital talent is more focused on the security of their job and expects their company to make the required efforts for keeping their job in place. Digital talent with more years of seniority in a certain company is more focused on learning and development and expects their company to provide them with professional and personal development opportunities that reflect their career and personal goals. Moreover, a change in the position or in the assigned project may determine a switch from one frame to another; therefore, when digital talent faces changes in their job role, their focus switches toward the novice motivation frame. Companies' awareness of individual motivation frames is critical for identifying the practices that best fit the particular needs of digital talent in order to boost their attraction to and development within a company, which are expected to lead to greater job satisfaction and an increased organizational commitment and retention.

References

Bidwell, M. J. (2011). Paying More to Get Less: The Effects of External Hiring Versus Internal Mobility. *Administrative Science Quarterly, 56*(3), 369–407.

Björkman, I., Ehrnrooth, M., Mäkelä, K., & Sumelius, J. (2017). Talent Management in Multinational Corporations. In D. G. Collings, K. Mellahhi, & W. F. Cascio (Eds.), *The Oxford Handbook of Talent Management*. Oxford University Press.

Caligiuri, P., Tarique, I., & Jacobs, R. (2009). Selection for International Assignments. *Human Resource Management Review, 19*(3), 251–262.

Chaudhuri, S., Hirudayaraj, M., & Ardichvili, A. (2018). Borrow or Grow: An Overview of Talent Development/Management Practices in Indian IT Organizations. *Advances in Developing Human Resources, 20*(4), 460–478.

Farndale, E., Pai, A., Sparrow, P., & Scullion, H. (2014). Balancing Individual and Organizational Needs During an International Assignment: A Mutual-Benefits Perspective. *Journal of World Business, 49*(2), 204–214.

Minbaeva, D., & Vardi, S. (2019). Global Talent Analytics. In D. G. Collings, H. Scullion, & P. Caligiuri (Eds.), *Global Talent Management* (2nd ed.). Routledge.

PWC. (2017). *2017 CEO Pulse Survey*. PwC.

Ready, D. A., & Peebles, M. E. (2015). Developing the Next Generation of Enterprise Leaders. *MIT Sloan Management Review, 57*(1), 43–51.

Sparrow, P., & Makram, H. (2015). What is the value of talent management? Building value-driven processes within a talent management architecture. *Human Resource Management Review, 25*(3), 249–263.

CHAPTER 5

Conclusion: Digital Talent Management—Into the Age of Renewal

Abstract This chapter concludes by bringing together the main arguments of the book and by outlining their implications for research and practice. It first summarizes the contribution that this book makes to the existing literature by defining and developing the concept of digital talent and delineating digital talent management (DTM) as a human-centered talent management process that consists of strategies and practices applied and applicable to digital talent. Further, this chapter discusses the managerial implications of this research by emphasizing how a crisis such as COVID-19 has impacted the management of digital talent. It ends with a look into the future of DTM in post-COVID-19 times—a future that is both uncertain and unalike what the world has witnessed before.

Keywords Digital talent • Digital talent management (DTM) • Post-COVID-19

We started working on this book when we realized that there is more to the vast array of professionals and managers who work in today's dynamic, innovative and knowledge-intensive industries that rely on digital competencies and skills—what we call 'digital talent'—than customarily believed. To a certain degree, we wanted to do justice to these talented individuals, who are all too often misrepresented in the popular culture, by outlining their 'idiosyncrasies', while showing the variety, differences and

S. Dan et al., *Digital Talent Management*,
https://doi.org/10.1007/978-3-030-76750-1_5

contributions they bring to our economies and society. Digital talent is about software developers and coding, but also about much more than just this. Turning to the academic literature on talent management and digital work proved useful as it enabled us to flesh out and anchor our own thinking about the distinctiveness and development of this dynamic spectrum of professionals and managers. Yet, we found that there are missing specifications in the existing literature when it comes to understanding who digital talent is, as distinctive individuals who find themselves in some of the most competitive industries of the global economy. These research gaps first provided us with the opportunity to develop the concept of digital talent. We put this idea into practice by proposing a human-centered approach to defining and managing talent that incorporates both the attributes of digital talent that are shared with other knowledge-intensive professions and their distinctiveness as individual human beings. Second, the identified research gaps allowed us to delineate, based on existing, yet disconnected streams of research on talent management and digital work (i.e., research on knowledge workers generally and information and communication technology, or IT&C, professionals specifically), a set of strategies and practices that form digital talent management (DTM). We understand DTM to be a human-centered talent management process that takes into account the distinctive nature of digital talent and is applicable to organizations that operate across different industries and sectors that undergo a digital transformation process. This includes the IT&C industry, which has experience in managing digital talent, but goes beyond it to include other industries that are subject to digital transformation and require digital competencies and skills.

Moreover, we suggested that digital talent can be understood at different levels of analysis depending on the types of actors and scope of activities that are included in the analysis and, more generally, in digitalization and digital transformation processes. In a narrow sense and in line with the bulk of the existing literature, digital talent includes technical implementers—the digital experts who develop software through coding. However, our argument is that this classification leaves out other actors who perform digital activities, roles and tasks and contribute in significant ways to the digital transformation of different industries, not only the IT&C industry. These roles include product/service managers, but also leaders of organizations and the inventors and creators who generate an idea that may subsequently become a new digital product/service. Digital expertise is required in order to carry out these processes. All these actors contribute, in one way or another, to designing, developing and/or implementing digital innovations, possess digital abilities, competencies and skills and are part of digital transformation, although they are not necessarily and exclusively employed by organizations operating in the IT&C industry. Due to their contributions to digitalization processes, they are digital talent in a broad sense. Therefore, in this broad sense, we defined digital talent as individuals who contribute to digitalization and digital transformation processes, regardless of their organizational form and structure, across different industries and sectors in one or more of the following ways: inventing/creating an idea that may subsequently become a new digital product/service; contributing, within a specific organizational setting, to one or more stages of the new digital product/service development process from concept/ideation to manufacture/launch and improvement; or leading an entity or activity, regardless of its organizational features, through which one or more of these roles, activities and tasks are carried out.

Despite the fact that digital talent constitutes a variety of professionals and managers and carries out a wide spectrum of activities, roles and tasks, much of the existing academic literature focuses on IT&C professionals in a narrow sense with reference to technical implementers who typically include computer programmers and software developers who write code. We addressed this observation through a more thorough definition and presentation of different types of IT&C professionals and managers reflecting this approach. Following this contribution, based on the empirical research reported in this volume, we then inductively developed a working definition of digital talent. This definition followed the standard stages of a new product development (NPD) process and reflected a more limited set of actors than outlined in the first definition above. Using this approach, we defined digital talent as individuals who: possess and productively employ, to different degrees, a variety of innate and/or acquired digital abilities, competencies and skills; operate within an organizational setting within the IT&C industry; and are responsible for activities, roles and tasks that cover one or more stages of a new product development process.

Our second starting point was built on the first and revolved around the specific characteristics of digital talent and their implications for talent management generally and talent attraction, development and retention specifically. Considering that digital talent constitutes the engine of innovation and business development, it adds considerable value to organizations, economies and societies (Balthasar et al., 2010). The dynamism of knowledge-intensive industries, which are in constant need of expansion, coupled with labor shortages, means that digital talent enjoys a privileged position on the labor market worldwide. As a result, companies develop talent management programs that aim both to attract new digital talent and increase existing digital talent's job satisfaction in order to nurture talent, reduce costly turnover and improve organizational commitment and retention (George, 2015). For these reasons, we chose to center our focus on the organizational implications of attracting, developing and retaining digital talent. Since our empirical research coincided with the outbreak and worldwide spread of COVID-19, it allowed us to understand these implications in this atypical context that has had a significant impact on corporate financial results, work arrangements, productivity and well-being, as well as digital talent management specifically. We showed that the specific characteristics of digital talent pose management challenges for organizations that need to ensure that one of their most valuable resources—their digital talent—chooses to remain within the organization or continue to do business with the organization through alternative retention mechanisms, such as building partnerships and jointly developing start-ups within the same ecosystem. In this way, organizations lose talent only in part to the extent that digital talent who opts for such alternative arrangements continues to contribute to the development of the same business or ecosystem.

The empirical evidence presented in this book brings to the fore insights regarding the challenges and strategies that IT&C companies use in order to remain competitive and manage digital talent effectively and efficiently. COVID-19 has intensified existing challenges and accelerated the development of talent management practices. Based on individual interviews with executives, HR staff and IT&C professionals, the book provided evidence on such strategies and highlighted their managerial implications. The new socio-economic context, influenced by the outbreak and spread of COVID-19, pushed companies in our sample to work in globally distributed teams and to further automatize and digitalize many of their core processes, which put pressure on digital talent management. In order to understand how to overcome these challenges, it is essential to show how the external context and internal organizational factors have influenced digital talent management. In order to remain competitive and to attract new projects, companies are redefining their own human resource strategies while adapting to environmental pressures.

Our research further points to the following specific findings: first, organizational digital talent management strategies and practices vary depending on the characteristics of digital talent, and professional experience is a recurring characteristic. Our evidence shows that experienced digital talent with a higher level of seniority within the organization is focused on and motivated by learning and development, work-life balance and well-being, while junior-level digital talent is more interested in financial benefits, work conditions and job security.

Second, flexible work arrangements are needed to become even more flexible during COVID-19. Digital talent expects the possibility to opt for work-from-home arrangements, with flexible hours, and expect a high level of job autonomy. The advantages of a high degree of job autonomy are twofold. Digital talent's job satisfaction is expected to increase, which leads to greater engagement, while companies benefit from the increased responsibilities taken up by their digital talent. However, these work arrangements require the adjustment of management approaches, complemented by e-leadership practices.

Third, talent attraction and development can function as early and ongoing retention strategies. By integrating these classic functions of talent management, companies can better succeed in retaining their digital talent. A good recruitment strategy, focused on transparency and clear information about the job profile, ensures a better match between newcomers' abilities and skills and job requirements. Transparent recruitment represents an early retention strategy, contributing to increased chances for the digital talent to remain longer in the company. Thus, a focus on talent development may directly contribute to improved retention. By offering development opportunities, companies help digital talent feel accomplished and support their continuous growth. In this way, both talent attraction and development can contribute to digital talent retention over the long term.

These findings lead to a series of managerial implications. In times of change, digital talent management is critical. Having the right talent in-house can 'make or break' the success of an organization even more so than in non-critical times. Therefore, our findings suggest that it is helpful for companies to launch a proactive communication approach so that digital talent feels close to the employer and their manager. At the same time, organizations and managers need to have an approachable attitude to ease interaction and create a sense of mutual understanding and consideration. Moreover, it helps if the consequences of COVID-19, including both risks and new opportunities, are presented and explained in a clear, yet thoughtful way. In this way, digital talent can understand the implications, or lack thereof, for the implementation of measures that aimed at protecting the company's financial results. This communication can address possible digital talent demotivation, which can stem from the companies' inability to sustain or increase their labor costs. Such strategy can result in greater organizational satisfaction and commitment, and reduced turnover. In order to sustain their financial results, IT&C companies resorted to cost-saving measures, but at the same time, they took concrete steps in order to preserve the commitment of their digital talent. These practices have contained different approaches and measures depending on the following two main factors:

- The maturity and cohesion of the companies' organizational culture;
- The way in which the management understood to carry out a sustained process of digital talent engagement concerning the creation of value added during difficult times.

In addition to focusing on e-leadership and ensuring good communication with individual digital talent, understanding their particular perspective can go a long way toward improving digital talent's well-being and retention over the medium and long term. We highlight that a one-size-fits-all management approach is likely to fail in motivating digital talent, and particular preferences and needs ought to be addressed as a function of digital talent's personal characteristics, such as professional expertise, career development goals and work-life needs. Moreover, implementing an integrated digital talent management approach that consists of a flow and interplay between attraction, development and retention is likely to be more effective than a piecemeal approach that ignores and leaves out one or more of these inter-related functions. Depending on organizational specificities, offering a compelling digital talent value proposition, developing a premium employer brand, flexible work arrangements, job autonomy, providing attractive development opportunities, benefits and modern working conditions with access to facilities and equipment for telework represent some of the strategies employers could focus on and adopt for successfully managing digital talent. Our research findings further suggest that alternative practices used by IT&C companies, such as supporting the development of an ecosystem of partners able to deliver specialized expertise, can facilitate digital talent management and address temporary talent shortages.

What does the future hold? What are organizations required to do in the future in order to successfully design and implement digital talent management? How can they adapt to an uncertain context and overcome the competitive pressures placed on their most talented professionals and managers? In times of COVID-19, it has been often claimed that digitalization has become the watchword of the global economy. This idea rests upon the premise that as a whole knowledge-intensive industries, such as the IT&C industry, benefit significantly during and in the aftermath of crises. However, we found that most companies included in our sample had already gone through an accelerated digitalization process over the past years. These processes were intensified under COVID-19 and are expected to go further during the coming years.

Furthermore, digital talent management strategies are likely to be even more closely connected with a convincing digital talent value proposition, employer branding and use of social media recruitment platforms. Professional recruitment platforms allow recruiters to rapidly identify suitable candidates. New practices include the use of algorithms and artificial intelligence (AI) tools as part of recruitment processes. Established recruitment practices are complemented by alternative approaches, such as freelancing and short-term commitments, frequently used in the gig economy (Prassl, 2018). An important aspect concerning the use of digital talent recruitment and selection consists of creating a positive recruitment and selection experience early on. This includes adopting alternative interview platforms that may convince talented candidates to join a certain organization. Talent attraction is also closely connected to induction. Evidence shows that effective induction hinges on a clear onboarding process that is easily modifiable and reflects the needs of new recruits. The induction and onboarding process is further influenced by promotion and communication activities and the degree of organizational and managerial support (Rodeghero et al., 2020).

Given digital talent's specific work environment, their enhanced mobility and competitive labor market pressures, the importance of talent development strategies is expected to grow over the coming years in order to ensure digital talent's organizational commitment. Taking into consideration digital talent's professional autonomy and preference for flexible work arrangements, companies need to adopt development strategies that target retention, including career planning and professional development, performance appraisal and motivation, and the use of a variety of rewards and recognition schemes that are tailored to individual preferences. Post-COVID-19 times are expected to be different in terms of work arrangements but not significantly and immediately different than the pandemic context in terms of digital talent's well-being. This implies that companies need to continue to invest in implementing supportive measures that aim to address individual and collective well-being.

As we look into the future, far beyond COVID-19, it is important to stress that crises do not only involve costs and risks, but they can also create new opportunities and can constitute a stimulus for organizational change. This can take the form of an authentic transformation of organizational structures and processes. Such deep learning can result in a transition toward adopting fluid and agile ways of operating by simplifying and automatizing all processes, structures and interactions, from sales to delivery and business support. For example, one of the most innovative sales practices used by the companies analyzed in our research was the development of a 'customer experience room'. Through this customer experience room, customers have the opportunity to virtually experience the organization by meeting sales representatives and software engineers who have the skills required for the development of new projects. In this innovative way, customers are also introduced to the organization's culture. Internal business support processes need to be part of this transition, which may include:

- Effective tools for sourcing and online recruitment;
- Adopting new communication tools, which better suit each project objective and the organizational culture;
- Building new training and development platforms;
- Ensuring talent coaching sessions, which can be a good strategy to overcome both professional and personal challenges that impact digital talent's well-being and productivity;
- Organizing regular meetings with the CEO and other board members in order to discuss current projects' status and present new organizational strategies;
- Using new motivation practices related to career development, learning opportunities, performance recognition, work flexibility and digital talent well-being;
- Adopting innovative practices such as a 'technology radar' initiative in order to assess the development of new technologies, which can

align the organization with the market opportunities and further develop digital talent skills.

Moreover, telework could be reinvented into a hybrid model which includes both work from home and in office. To support this model, further automation of some operational processes may be required, such as time-tracking, holiday application or activity tracking. This can free up managers' time, which could be more productively invested in digital talent management. Nevertheless, we suggest that successful companies of the future will need to be prepared not only to redesign and incrementally change these organizational practices, but also to transform their organizational culture more deeply. Redefining their own culture and values means adopting a new inside-out concept, centered on collaboration, which is key to an increasingly digitalized world.

Finally, business as usual could be replaced with practices that may lead to better talent management to the extent that companies prioritize digital talent's well-being. The companies' efforts could center on aligning factors known to have a direct bearing on well-being, such as clarity of responsibilities, workload, work-life balance, interference of family stress with work and individual characteristics that impact digital talent performance, including goal setting, planning and efficacy. However, essential to this approach is the support provided by the organization as a whole and/or direct managers, who find themselves in the best position to know digital talent personally and to know them well. Having this in mind is, in our opinion, the single most important factor influencing the success of digital talent management.

References

Balthasar, A., Bättig, C., Thierstein, A., & Wilhelm, B. (2010). "Developers": Key Actors of the Innovation Process: Types of Developers and Their Contacts to Institutions Involved in Research and Development, Continuing Education and Training, and the Transfer of Technology. *Technovation, 20*, 523–538.

George, C. (2015). Retaining Professional Workers: What Makes Them Stay? *Employee Relations, 37*(1), 102–121.

Prassl, J. (2018). *Humans as a Service: The Promise and Perils of Work in the Gig Economy*. Oxford: Oxford University Press.

Rodeghero, P., Zimmermann, T., Houck, B., & Ford, D. (2020). *Please Turn Your Cameras On: Remote Onboarding of Software Developers During a Pandemic*. Retrieved January 15, 2021, from https://arxiv.org/pdf/2011.08130v1.pdf

Index

S. Dan et al., *Digital Talent Management*,
https://doi.org/10.1007/978-3-030-76750-1

The manufacturer's authorised representative in the EU is Springer Nature Customer Service Centre GmbH, Europaplatz 3, 69115 Heidelberg, Germany. If you have any concerns regarding our products, please contact ProductSafety@springernature.com

Printed and bound by CPI Group (UK) Ltd, Croydon, CR0 4YY
25/09/2026
02223153-0002